Commercial Real estate Investing & Business Management For beginners & Expert

ENTERPRISE STRATEGIC POLICY AND INTERIOR PLANNING DESIGN TO PROFIT YOUR COMMERCE

L. KELLER

CONTENTS

COMMERCIAL REAL ESTATE INVESTOR FOR BEGINNERS

STARTUP AND BUSINESS MANAGEMENT

COMMERCIAL REAL ESTATE INVESTING FOR BEGINNERS

L. KELLER

INTR O DUCTIO N

Real estate: everyone is talking about it. It looks like we all know someone who knows someone who has become very successful thanks to it. Unfortunately, because of how profitable it can be, people often classify it as one of those businesses for rich people rather than what it actually is: one of those business that make people rich. If you have decided to venture into the world of real estate, have a seat. Thanks to this book, dedication, and your willpower, you will carve a nice place for yourself in the real estate world. This is the best thing about real estate; there is enough room for as many as are interested.

Before you can effectively make anything out of this world, you have to understand it completely. Real estate does not favor impulsive businessmen or people who do not have a sufficient knowledge. Before doing anything, you must study.

What Is Commercial Real Estate?

Real estate simply deals with possession of land and buildings. When the word 'commercial' is thrown in, there is usually a bit of confusion. People ask "Isn't all real estate commercial? Isn't business always involved? Isn't the aim to make money?". These questions are valid but, however, the explanation is simple. In real estate, buildings and lands are leased, sold, bought, and rented. The business transaction could be between the seller (who is called a realtor) and individuals or between the realtor and business organizations. When it comes to individuals, there could be several reasons for the sale. However, if it is between realtors and business organizations, we are talking about buying, renting or leasing a workspace. Commercial real estate refers to business deals concerning properties that are meant for business purposes. When commercial real estate is mentioned, you need to know that the concerned property is not for personal use. When it comes to living spaces, it is known as residential real estate.

Just like residential real estate, commercial real estate is divided into four categories. These categories are:

- **Office**: This refers to buildings that will be used as an office of any sort.
- **Multifamily**: Multifamily homes are homes that allow more than a single person to live there so that the collection of rent becomes a business itself.
- **Retail**: This refers to buildings that were built and designed for retail purposes. These include supermarkets, shops, and other retail business.
- **Industrial**: these spaces refer to buildings used to produce goods.

The industrial building is further divided into three classes:

- **Class A**: This class refers to buildings that are based on age or quality and have a certain aesthetic value attached to it. These buildings are highly valued and very competitive. They are the ones that have good locations and other qualities that make it attractive.
- **Class B**: Class B buildings are aged buildings that do not attract as many people and are therefore not as competitive as Class A buildings due to the prices attached to them. There is less competition where prices are concerned. These buildings are usually marked out for restoration.
- **Class C**: Buildings which fall into this category are usually old. Averagely, they are over twenty years of age. Due to their age, they require maintenance. They are also located in areas that are not attractive.

It is very important to familiarize with these terms and classes.

CHAPTER 1: WHAT YOU SHOULD KNOW ABOUT COMMERCIAL REAL ESTATE

You need to know that real estate is more than just being a landlord. Most people don't have the correct idea. We think about the problems and stresses we give to our landlords and we assume that that is the definition of investing in real estate. Real estate is not for everyone, agreed. However, before you decide that it is what you want to do, you should know what it is and what to expect. Getting deterred by the fear of the unknown is one of the surest ways never to make profits or to succeed.

When you invest in commercial real estate, you open the possibility for higher yields. When you have a building in an area, the profit that you will get from it depends on how much traffic that area receives. Think of yourself as a businessman who is trying to get his business out there. You decide to rent a place and you have two options. The first is in an area with a high population. That area has a lot of people passing through it. In the second area, life is more slow-paced and reserved and the population is not as good as the previous one. Which out of those two options would you pick? Normally, you would pick the first option since there is a higher chance of people being able to discover your business. Thus, even if the price of that building is higher, it would seem fair to you and you would not mind paying for that. This is one of the reasons why prices vary and differ.

If you have a property for sale in a student-area and a pizza shop wants to purchase it, you should know what your building can offer them. Residential tenants are less bound to this.

One other advantage of stepping into the scene of real estate in the commercial setting is that it is generally easier for you as a person. A tenant living residentially may choose to ignore small defects. If they can live with them, they will ignore them even though they will only get worse. However, most business would prefer fixing even the smallest defects to give their building a better image. There are also various improvements that business owners would carry out on the property. For instance, your tenant decides to improve the wiring system in order to enhance his business. When he leaves, he won't take the wiring with him. The value of your property would then increase.

Generally, it is even easier to rent out to businesses. Take collection of rents as an example. Usually, most business pay their rents on time. That payment is usually budgeted and considered first. They will not want to risk losing the building. However, in the case of residential real estate, it is very common to encounter resistance when it comes to collecting rents. It is easier for a person to run away in order to avoid rents than for a company to do that.

How Does Investing In Commercial Real Estate Work?

The logic behind commercial real estate is very easy to understand. Every office space or commercial building is a product of commercial real estate. There is more than one way to make money off it. When commercial real estate is mentioned, a lot of people let their minds slip to rents, and that is all. That means being close minded. It is true that to engage in commercial real estate you need more funds, but that also has a whole plethora of advantages attached to it. Since the aim of commercial real estate is to help make profit and not to provide a place to rest one's head, the customers involved are usually objective for what they can gain from your location. Finding that out gets you an edge. No good businessman will decide to rent out a space for his business without knowing very well what he can gain from it.

The risks attached to commercial real estate can be very attractive if one plays his cards right. It is also one of the easiest ways one can have a diversified portfolio. Commercial real estate is not a one-way street. There are several ways through which one can make a profit. These are ways that are not available when investing in residential real estate.

How Profitable is Real Estate Marketing?

It goes without saying that real estate is perhaps one of the most profitable businesses that one can go into. Generally, real estate investors report various levels and amounts of returns on their investments. The amount of profit you get actually depends on the type of investment you engage in. For example, the average return on investment associated with residential real estate is pinned at an average of 10.6% annually. On the other hand, commercial properties rack in somewhat higher profits. The average is pinned at 12% which raises it a notch higher than residential real estate. However, this really depends on what you do and on how you do it.

Commercial Real Estate As A Passive Income

A passive income is a way of earning money that does not depend on how much time you spend working. Often times, we find that we are not really being paid for our skills but for our time. However, there is so much time in a day and out of those available hours, there is a maximum we can use. A passive income does not depend on those hours you spend working. Of course, at the initial stage, your time would be greatly required in order to start it up. However, once you are not a novice anymore, the following steps will depend on how well you did in the initial stages. Time will then begin to work for you and not the other way around.

Real estate – commercial real estate in particular – is a very good way to passively earn a living. Passive income building is becoming more and more important as the years go by. Jobs are no longer solid and, if you want to be objective, having a side option is a smart thing. For one thing, a passive income can actually fund your retirement plan. You can focus on your active income plan while your passive income plans the life you will have after that. Your passive income can help you save money, increase your financial strength, grow your savings, or you can even decide to face it directly and dump your active income sources.

If you want to dump your active income, you will need to diversify. This means that you will probably need to have more than one source of passive income. That way, you are not at risk, which is the whole point of having a passive income. Having multiple streams of income also has some benefits when it comes to taxes. Normally, we pay taxes on ordinary income, investment or portfolio income, and passive income. Money gotten from real estate would definitely classify as investment or portfolio income. This type of income is not taxed so highly which is amazing, considering what you can do with it.

There are four strategies that you need to know in order to make a passive income from commercial real estate.

Crowdfunding

Real estate crowdfunding is a new way that real estate investors are using to make money. If you are accredited as an investor, you can engage in funding a real estate property. You can take a place as one of several investors who will come together to contribute in order to enable a third-party to buy and even control and manage an investment property. The proceeds from such will differ depending on the property purchased and the amount contributed. This comes down to the arranged structure for sharing profits. You could be paid monthly, quarterly, biannually, or annually. The success of crowdfunding depends on whoever the investor is, and this is why you must consider it very carefully.

Rental property

This is an obvious way that everyone knows. Most people have a knowledge of real estate that is limited to rental properties. There are so many ways to rent out commercial properties. The general idea is to rent a property to a business or organization that would pay you rent. Whatever rent that tenant pays to you should definitely be more than the amount you spent on the building. If every month you are paid $1,300 and you find that you pay $300 every month in expense, it means you are actually earning $1000 each month. Most people have caretakers that take care of the responsibilities that renting out presents. It is usually better to delegate as much as you can while still making a profit. That way, you do not tie yourself down ad block out other possible streams.

REIT dividend

REIT stands for Real Estate Investment Trust. REIT refers to companies that are publicly or privately traded. These companies gather money from investors in order to buy and manage multiple commercial real estate properties. Then, they pay at least 90% of the income that is taxable to shareholders. This way, the dividend return is higher than most other stocks.

The cost of this is quite low since other investors are also involved in this. The returns they provide are very much worth it. The income from this is not taxed as a passive income. Rather, it is taxed as portfolio income.

Performing mortgage notes

Most people have never heard of what it means to perform a mortgage note. An income can be made by buying or creating a mortgage note. It is quite advanced, a little complicated and therefore not as popular. Although a low number of people involve themselves in it, those who do swear by it.

Notes and mortgages have similar meanings and duties, although they are two different documents. A buyer is loaned money to buy real estate and is given the note and mortgage as documents or contracts. It is in the note that the payments schedule will be outlined. The debt will be repaid in an agreed method and the note will have the details of it. The mortgage, on the other hand, is a form of security given to the lender in case the borrower/buyer does not meet up with the agreed terms in the note.

At a specified time, each month, the borrower or buyer pays the lender a principle and interest payment. It is the borrower that will maintain the property and pay all taxes as well as insurance while the lender only collects his payments when due and keeps records.

The most common and easy method of making money through real estate is by renting and leasing, so you should pay large attention to it. The whole essence of engaging in real estate is to make money in a passive way in order to give you an option to fall back on.

Why Invest In Commercial Real Estate?

Commercial real estate is not the only way to make a passive income. It seems to require a lot, so a lot of people wonder why exactly they should try it out. Here there are some of the primary reasons why you should invest in commercial real estate:

Diversification

A lot of people try to diversify because they do not want to put all their eggs in one basket. This is not only smart; it is also very important. There are various ways to diversify. One can diversify through stocks, bonds, and other methods. Why real estate? Well, real estate has several behavioral patterns that you would not find in other passive incomes. For one thing, a drop in stock prices does not affect the fact that people would still need businesses. As one business runs bankrupt, another starts up. As more jobs are created, more office spaces are needed. It is one of the safest ways to diversify. It is also one of the passive incomes that require the least presence.

Improved Cash Flow

Commercial real estate is not just about the present. If great decisions are made, one would definitely know that the possibility of appreciation in the future is great. If you collect rents, you know that the rents are a great percentage of whatever it is that you earn. Once rent is fixed, it will not come down except in the event that the tenant moves out, and if it is located a hot area, there will even be competition for it. The income will be regular and having a regular income allows planning and budgeting to expand and grow.

Less Volatility

Volatility refers to the measurement of uncertainty about the price of a financial instrument. Stock and bond prices are attached with high volatility. Unlike any other type of real estate, commercial real estate usually involves long-term agreements. Usually, they sign an agreement from 3 to 5 years. The fact that it is longer reduces volatility greatly. Some leases even extend to longer periods of time. For whatever period that a lease is signed, you have a large modicum of assurance of receiving a particular sum of money for a pretty long time. The fact that real estate is publicly traded further reduces the volatility. Having a sense of security added to your financial instruments helps one to plan ahead and make decisions based on accredited foresight.

Physical Assets

Unlike several other financial tools, hard assets are more solid. If you follow stock prices, you realize that the value placed on them is determined by demand and supply. This means that news or events may sink a stock that was doing very well. They are not physical, and this means that they can become worthless within the blink of an eye. This means that the intrinsic value of real estate is deeply rooted in both the building and the land. That cannot disappear. Sure, it can get devalued but the rate and risk of that happening can be avoided and reduced. It is harder to go wrong in real estate than in stocks. Once you get the hang of real estate, you are bound to make less mistakes. Ambitious assets can be changed to increase value. A drop in prices is never as sudden as in stocks.

Potential Tax Benefits

In the case of several events, there are various tax benefits to be claimed. Events such as interest expense, depreciation, and various other things attract that tax deductions.

Take, for example, the fact that IRS allows commercial real estate investors to reduce a portion of a property's depreciated value. This is in a bid to help account for the expenses gotten from maintenance as well as upkeep. There are various tax laws that allow for a deduction in taxes.

Presence of Insurance

Because of the nature of stocks and bonds, it is hardly ever possible to be completely protected by insurance. At best, you can hedge. Hedging is a method used to protect yourself, it does not block the investor from negative steps. Rather, it provides a plan B if that happens. From the explanation, it is obvious that it does not mean being fully protected. Insurance, on the other hand, is different. If a natural disaster or any other type of accident occurs, your insurance can pay for it. The presence of insurance makes the possibilities of risk even lower for the investor.

Of course, the main reason why you should invest in commercial real estate is that it is a very passive way to make money. If you have been wishing for an escape from your ordinary financial cycle, this could be the answer for you. Luckily, thanks to the way it is set up, you can hire out most work required and still make profits. People will always want to start up business. There will always be new ideas that are yet to be actualized. Commercial buildings will always be in need, and when you enter a business which involves supplying something that will be needed forever, you know that you are on the right track.

Commercial real estate offers a financial freedom that many crave. From it, empires have been built. The fact that it gives a bit of assurance of a profitable future makes it hot cake. Of course, one needs to put in a lot of effort at the initial stage. But when the right amount of capital is put in, success is guaranteed.

Historically, real estate has performed beautifully over the years. It has shown very great yield and has steadily proven to be a good investment. It has outperformed both stocks and bonds, which is no surprise. The growth it has shown has been steady and very stable. Of course, this does not mean that it is immune to changes and that it cannot be affected by general lows such as inflation. It just means that it has proven to be able to take a hit much better. The growth which it experiences is not predicted to stop anytime soon. In fact, it is predicted to improve in the forthcoming years.

Why Do Some Real Estate Business Fail?

From what we have discussed so far, the world of commercial real estate might seem like rainbows and sunshine. It may sound like it is impossible to fail. It seems straightforward with a lot of precautionary methods. You may even have the thought that failure is rare or impossible. It is time to drop that thought. A lot of people fail at real estate. Sure, the introductory part sounds easy and fun. However, as we go deeper, it will be noticeable why it is so easy for a lot of people to fail. But now you can look at the failure of others to know the things that you should not do. In this chapter, we will be looking at some of the most common reasons why people fail at real estate:

They Do Not Have The Right Mindset

There are several reasons why real estate investors fail. However, one of the most common reasons is the way they think. The attitude you have towards a thing will affect your performance greatly. A lot of real estate investors are not confident enough to make decisions. Sometimes, we make good decisions, but we end up second-guessing ourselves so much that we change our mind when we shouldn't. When someone starts out on the journey of real estate, he is usually optimistic. Of course, he knows he will encounter some problems but when the problems come, it is usually not in the area where he expected it. Sometimes, the problems he faces cause losses, and because of that he starts to lose confidence in himself. Pessimism steps in and when that happens, it is game over. When an investor doubts himself or herself, they stop putting in so much because, consciously or unconsciously, they feel that they cannot succeed and reach what they are craving.

Poor Work on Listings

A lot of real estate agents do not take the time to create appealing listings. Your listing can greatly affect the success of your business. Of course, there are some buildings in areas that do not need listings. This is because they are so popular that the moment they are vacated, new tenants are lining up. Ideally, that is the sort of property every real estate investor wants but, actually, we do not always get it. It is your listing that will make your available building look as attractive as possible. Think of your listing as the first way to attract buyers. In your listing, information must be presented accurately and enticingly. A listing is not a place to exaggerate the perfection of the place. Rather, it is an opportunity to highlight the good sides in a very realistic way. If you do not channel everything you have into your listings, your property will stay on the market for much longer than it should and that would contribute to the downfall of your business. Take time to create the perfect listing. I strongly believe that if you make it through your first year successfully, you will excel. The first year is the hardest. It is a time for mistakes, learning, and even more mistakes. However, if one makes too many mistakes, it is understandable that they will want to give up. That is why everyone should work very hard during the fist year.

They Underestimate Hard Work

Sure, it is important to have the right mindset. Of course, the knowledge and tools you have also matter. But even with all these things, you might barely scale through. Without hard work, you have no chance of succeeding. A passive income requires that you lay a very good foundation in order to reap benefits. When you go into a business newly, hard work is as important as your knowledge. A lot of new real estate investors do not work hard enough. They channel their energy into other things. Like I said, in the first year, hard work is extremely important. Successful real estate investors have invested hours of their time into it before resting back to watch their fruits ripen. While setting it up, you must put all into it and know that in a while, you will enjoy it. When starting out, the hours might be tough, but it helps when we remind ourselves that it is only for the beginning. Talk to a successful real estate investor that you know. Ask how many hours he or she spent to set things up and you will realize that in order to earn a passive income, hard work must have been sowed.

They Do Not Fully Understand Real Estate

The sad thing about real estate is that since it is often associated to rich and powerful people, many have wrong assumptions about it. These rich and powerful people usually have their hands in a lot of passive incomes, and we assume that they simply sit and relax while money is made. That makes us think that if we also enter the business, it would be that easy to make money. Can real estate make a lot of money? Yes! Is it easy? No! You should know what exactly you can make and what you will need in order to make it. Real estate is a business and not a money doubling avenue. The glamorous lives or stories you see only cover a part of the main deal. Do not expect to enjoy it immediately. There are so many advantages when investing in real estate. Think about how it can make a brighter future for you and how it can give you a modicum of financial security. Go in for the right reasons and you will have no problems.

They Expect Profits Right Away

The fact that money comes in right away does not mean that profits will come in. Imagine if you spend a total of a $100 in acquiring a property and making it ready for renting. Let's say that your first tenant pays $10 each month. The fact is that monthly, a portion of money comes in. However, that is not yet profit. Most people do not consider this. Another thing is that even when you have a landed property on ground that is ready to be rented, it might take quite a while before one gets tenants. That period of waiting and searching can be quite discouraging, especially if you are a newbie. If you go into real estate expecting to roll in cash right away, the reality will disappoint you. However, for those who are diligent enough to wait patiently until their business is built, they will experience the great and rosy side of commercial real estate.

They Partner with The Wrong People

The problem with partnering with the wrong people is that having one bad team member can spoil everything you have built. As a commercial real estate investor, you will need to partner and network with various people who will help your business grow. Real estate agents, for example, are some of such people. However, just as one would expect, there are good ones and there are bad ones. If your team is full of people that are simply after their own personal gain, you will find that they will destroy your dream rather than help you build it. Whoever you are going to partner with must have a like minded aim and must understand your needs. You should not partner with people who do not carry you along. As you grow, you will meet other commercial real estate investors that will be as invested in your goal as you are. Those are the persons you should net-work with.

Hedging

When you think of a hedge, what comes to your mind? A protection of some sort? If that was your answer, you are right. Hedging has to do with a protection for investor's portfolios. Think of it as an investor's insurance although it operates in its own way.

When people get involved in the practice of hedging, they are protecting themselves against unforeseen negative occurrences. This is like what you do to a car or a house. You cannot predict the future and you do not want anything negative to happen to your portfolio and so you hedge it. Just as in insurance, it does not protect you from everything, but it is much better than nothing.

What is Hedging?

Hedging protects owners and managers of portfolios, investors, and even corporations. When you hedge, you strategically make use of your financial instrument to offset risks in the event that the price moves the way you did not plan to.

This means that you are literally taking a position that will support you if the actual outcome is the opposite of what you predicted. Hedging is paid purchasing a put option that will protect or shield you if a large negative movement occurs.

Hedging is much more precise than insurance. However, since hedging is not perfect, it is difficult to have an error-free one. Since risks are common and should not be overlooked, investors should do as much as they can to protect themselves. Hedging makes that opportunity available.

Risk management is an important part of any business. There are a lot of tips that investors will give you in order to help you make better decisions when it comes to protecting yourself against risk. Here are some of the best of those decisions that will help you reduce your risks.

Risk Management Tips:

Consider the Reward to Risk Ratio

When you perform analysis and spot a signal for entry, even before you place an order, think about where you want to take profits and where you intend to place your stop-loss order. As we have said before, commit it to your interface and not just in your head. Then measure the reward and risk ratio. Also, take into consideration how much you would be able to place on the trade with the 1 or 2% max in mind. Often times, you'll find out that it is not worth it. The risk should never be higher than the reward. If it does not look good for you, pass it over. Do not go looking for ways to put more in. There are always better trades. One thing a lot of people do is to come up with how much they want to put in and how much they want to get out. Then, they find a trade and try to place in stop-loss and take profit orders that fit what they want. But it does not work that way. The trade dictates. You do not dictate to the trade.

Avoid Fixed Stops That Do Not Consider Volatility

A lot of people suggest that traders make use of fixed stops for your stop-loss. But this is not advisable. Think of it as someone trying to make quick money. It is dangerous. You don't want to increase the risks in an already risky venture. It is riskier because momentum is not constant, and neither is volatility. This means that a number of certain prices will experience fluctuation. If the price didn't fluctuate, then the stock market would be very predictable. When you notice a higher volatility, set your stop-loss and your take profit accordingly. They should be wider in order to avoid losses and immature profits. When volatility is low, be sure to set them accordingly as well.

Try to Stay Away From Break-Even Stops

When you create a no-risk trade by moving your stop-loss very close to the entry point, you are caging yourself. Your profits could suffer tremendously. Do not over-protect yourself. These are mistakes you will not make if you analyze things properly. Especially as a swing trader, you should give yourself enough risk. Prices fluctuate; they go up and down. A stop-loss is good but do not place it too close to your entry.

Compare Your Win-rate

Yes, as some say, a win-rate is useless. Those who say so are right, but a win-rate is only useless if you look at it alone. The whole point is that a win-rate is not useless; it is not meant to be considered alone. If a trader ignores a win-rate, they are ignoring something that can provide very valuable insights. Your win-rate needs to be very high or you will have to hold on to trades for a while. If you have a win-rate of 40%, you are good to go if your reward:risk is higher than 1.6. Thanks to these stats, you are more likely to trade profitably.

Even if you try to get a very high win-rate or if you ride trades for a while, they will never be a guarantee.

Use Weekly Targets

As a swing trader, you should not be gauging your performance by the day. It keeps you short-sighted. To be able to properly analyze your performance, you need to consider the long run. It could also create a lot of pressure on you. Give yourself the time span of a week, not a day. On a daily scale, try to trade as best as you can. Put in everything you can into each trade. On a weekly scale, follow your rules. Work on your discipline. On a monthly or bi-monthly basis, be sure that you follow a professional routine. Now, you can review the mistakes you have made and come up with new lessons and rules to ensure that you will never make those mistakes again.

Make Use of the R-multiple

The R-multiple is used to measure your performance. It shows the results of your trades. You can consider the R-Multiple as well as the reward:risk ratio. The reward:risk ratio is the measurement that compares your reward and your risk. When you consider this, it gives you a realistic view of what it is that you are doing. Trade is not a place for extreme optimism. If you are optimistic, you have to have done something to back it up. If you compare the R-Multiple to your reward:risk, you'll have some new insights and you will be able to look for what caused the differences.

Pay Attention To Risk Management

In this book, we have spoken about various ways to manage risks. Stop-loss, take-profits, diversifying, etc. in their own way, each of them is very important. One should not take them for granted. They might look cumbersome, but it is much better to allow them to burden you now than to have to face several losses. Even the best traders make mistakes. This doesn't mean that they aren't professionals. It just shows the unpredictability of the market.

1. Keep an Evidence of Your Finances

   It is simple; you just need to keep track of your total income and enlist all your expenses. It let you have a sentiment of how much cash you can invest.

   However, do not assume that you will not be able to invest if you only have a small amount of cash available. You can sure get a loan if you have a firm job, a regular income, and a solid employment history.

2. Get a Pre-approval

   You should get a pre-approval through an experienced mortgage broker or a lender. However, if you are having any incertitude regarding your financial cognition to invest, then you must consult a broker before applying for pre-approval.

3. About Your Goals
   They are different from a real estate investor to another; set your goals along with a pragmatic deadline. A common mistake that you should avoid is setting goals that are too high or unrealistic.

4. Know the Risks
   Your strategy will be determined by your risk profile; be clear about the kind of risks that you are willing to take. Knowing your attitude towards risks will help you create your perfect scheme.

5. Budgeting
   Budgeting is the only mode to make sure that you have maintained and are going to maintain a constructive balance between your income and costs. Planning not only lets you know where your money is going, but it also helps you create a budjet for bigger expenses.

6. Investment Plan
   You cannot buy anything you want when it comes to real estate. You need to create a plan for your leverages so that you get the growth and returns you are aiming for.

7. Attention to the Latest Trends
   Keep following the latest way in the industry. There is no such thing as a one true method, the only thing that is going to help you succeed is keeping in touch with the industry and understanding the risks attached to it.
8. Stay focused and be patient
   An ordinary mistake that most commercial property buyers make while investing in real estate is letting their feelings interpose with their work. Always remember that you are making coherent decisions, not emotional ones.

If you keep learning and trying new plans of action; you will surely become successful.

CHAPTER 2: IT'S ALL IN YOUR MIND

If you have read through this book, congratulations. I am happy to tell you that almost nothing can defeat you now. Sure, you will encounter loss, but those losses will teach you all the lessons that you need. However, I saidalmost nothingcan defeat you. I hope you are wondering what it is that this extensive book did not cover. The answer is you Now, you are the only one who can defeat yourself. Even if you follow all the advice given in this book, you can still defeat yourself quite easily. How? Your feelings. Your greatest weaknesses are in your mind. Luckily, you can defeat them.

Dangerous Emotions

There are five emotions that can ruin you as a stock trader. The saddest part about this (and the most dangerous, too) is that emotions control us and so learning to control them is very hard. You may shrug and tell yourself: "After all, I'm not emotional, this isn't for me." Then you'd be wrong. If you have ever lost a very large sum of money even for a second, you know what panic feels like. You do not have to be emotional to feel certain things. Here are some emotions you should pay attention to:

Greed

How can we describe greed? Do you know that thought of wanting more? Well, that is not greed. That is the thirst that leads us to success. If there is no thirst or hunger to do something we have never done before, a lot of achievements would be merely dreams. The thing about thirst or hunger is that if you do not pay attention to them, they could turn into greed. Think of yourself as a fisherman who has been looking for means of income. Suddenly, he gets a boat, some tools and a good knowledge on how to fish. He has a nice captain that tends the boat while he drives. A few days ago, he had no food to eat. Today he's getting fish he can sell and eat. When he sees how profitable it is, he wakes up early to fish and does not go to bed until late. He does all of that because he has a thirst in him. However, when he starts to take 500 fish in his boat (that is meant for 400) to maximize his profits, he becomes greedy. He no longer wants to use nets, so he starts to electrocute fish in the water and take them out in larger numbers; he is greedy.

You could be that fisherman. When you start to put in more than 2% instead of trying to increase your spendable balance, you are getting greedy. When you make speedy analysis in order to take positions early, you are getting greedy. When you refuse to diversify and instead sink capital into one ground you feel will be fertile forever, you are greedy and greed will push you to make wrong decisions.

How To Guard Against Greed

The most efficient way to guard against greed is by making analysis and following your trading plan. It is your trading plan that will dictate what you have planned to do in a moment of critical thinking. You will collect profits when due and not later.

Fear

Fear is a terrible emotion. Maybe, it is one of the strongest. The fear of a killer will kill faster than the killer himself. Let's move back to our fisherman. He plans to go out to the deep end of the sea to get some rare fish and so he gets his gear ready and spends the required amount of time preparing. However, planning something and actually doing it are two different experiences. So, our fisherman enters the troubled seas. He sees the waves rising and he fears for his little boat. He wonders if it is safe out there. He questions his decision. He is thinking about the cost of his boat, of his equipment and his life. If he loses them, he'll go back to being a poor man and, even worse, he'll be in debt. And so, our fisherman decides to go back. He has just lost a lot of time.

You could also be that fisherman. Fear will make you lose faith in your own analysis. It is for this reason that we ask traders to be sure of their analysis. Fear will make you question all the rational decisions you have made. The worst thing is that fear is able to make you panic. Panic will make you give up faster than you should. Panic would make you jump out of a deal that was about to favor you. However, panic cannot set in without fear.

How To Guard Against Fear

The first thing you should do is to cover all bases. Your fear is smart if it pulls you out from a disastrous deal. But, if you cover all bases, you'll have the upper hand. Analyze everything patiently. However, that is not all. Each time you reach a conclusion, write it down on your trade journal along with the reason why you reached that conclusion. When fear wants to set in, those would be your comfort. Fear is deadly and when panic sets in, your ability to make rational decisions goes under attack. You do not want that to happen, and you should fight against it. Update your trade journal with all the details and analysis you need. They will help you put your mind at full rest.

Hope

We are often told to hope for the future. But in business, there is no room for hope. Analysis are not built on hope. They are built on rational thoughts and calculations. Let's think again about our fisherman. He steps out and sees it's a bad day. He has bought some fuel, a net, and some new gear. All those things cost money. But he sees the weather is bad. However, he has spent money and he doesn't want to lose it, so he starts to tell himself that the weather will get better. He is in it already and doesn't want to come out with a loss, so he tells himself to be patient. Raindrops pelt the boat, but he tells himself to be patient as the sun will soon shine and dry it up.

You could be the fisherman. You have analyzed your stop-loss point and you have it all picked out rightly. You do not give a stop-loss order, but you write it somewhere (that's your first mistake). When the loss sign hits, you develop hope and tell yourself that maybe, just maybe, it will rise up. Instead, it keeps sinking deeper and deeper until you lose more than you would have if you had obeyed the stop-loss.

How To Guard Against Undue Hope

In stock trade, hope should be the very last thing you add. Your right analysis should go first and then, you should obey the rules you have set for yourself and your trade. Nothing is more important. Write down your trade plan and stick to it.

Overconfidence

Overconfidence is the next deadly emotion. Overconfidence occurs when you let even small victories get to your head and feel that your victories are related to you and not to the work you put in. We have our fisherman again. This time, things are going well for him. He plans for five hours and brigs in a full boat. After a while, he starts to plan for four hours and when he sees that his boat is still full, he plans for two. However, that is not enough and so, one day, he spends so little time planning that he does not foresee a storm that wrecks his boat.

You could be just like the fisherman. You are not experiencing success because of who you are. You are doing it because of your work. When you get overconfident, you start to underestimate the value of work and of the preparation you put in. Hence, you will obtain poor results.

How To Guard Against Overconfidence

Have a trading routine and a trading plan. They are bound to keep you in check. You should follow your trading plan as a rule. Remember that you should first plan the trade and then trade the plan. During the trade, emotions are heightened, but you should only make the decisions that you have already set in your plan.

Regret

The last emotion is regret. Regret is an emotion that I will not class as bad. Regret itself is not bad, but what it triggers can be good or bad. For example, our fisherman realizes how silly he has been. He has gotten his boat damaged and now he will need to do some petty jobs in order to get money to fix it. The damage he has done is quite expensive, and he regrets not having paid more attention. If our fisherman decides to sell the remaining wood in his boat and give up, he has lost. But if he decides to analyze where he went wrong, pick out his mistakes, work on his analysis and be careful, he won't make the same mistakes twice.

How To Guard Against Regret

When things go wrong, especially when we realize we could have prevented it, regret is quite normal. However, it goes wrong when you allow it to drive you negatively. Perhaps you decide to trade riskily to win back your funds or perhaps you decide to give up. What happens might be slightly out of your control. When losses happen, reevaluate, learn, and pay attention to your mistakes, making sure never to make them again. Giving up is the actual loss.

CHAPTER 3: STEPS TO BUILD A TRADE PLAN

People sometimes think about trade plans but not everyone knows how to build one. Here are ten simple steps which could help you. A trading plan is where you write down every step that you take. I will answer the questions of what, where, and how. Then it will tell why.

1. Learn: What kind of knowledge do you lack? What is your feeling about not knowing? Learn from that. Acquire as much knowledge as possible.
2. Train yourself: Psychologically and financially train yourself, even emotionally. Have a clear mind. Do not go in with a negative mindset.
3. Write down some risk: Assess your account balance. Decide which percentage you want to risk. Note that you can even risk less than 1%. Only try to make sure you 're receiving more than $100 from commissions on any deal.
4. Set goals: Decide what you want to win and what you are looking for.
5. Analyze: Scan, analyze as much as you can technically and do research. Here is where you start preparing your trade. Get good reviews. The messages you get should be the ones you believe in the most. If they scare you, look for others. There are many out there.

6. Set the exit rules: When are you going to leave?
7. Set the entry rules: When is the best time to enter?
8. Document everything: Cleanly report everything. If anxiety threatens to pop up, it is this record that will hold you back.
9. Evaluate your performance: Evaluate your wins and losses. Learn from mistakes, and congratulate yourself when making the correct moves.

Routine; Why Is It Important?

You will need to get a new routine as a trader. As soon as you start it out it becomes part of you. They are not just routines for your business. They are for you, and for your life. You have to be at your best in order to trade, and that is why you need to have a routine. A man who had two hours of sleep, if he makes any profit at all, cannot enter the market and make as much profit as a well-rested man. You have to look after everything in your life. Here's an easy routine that you should adopt. You can customize it, of course, but make sure to keep the general idea.

1. Eat healthy food. Try not to work when you are hungry.
2. Look at the daily chart trend at the beginning of each week and describe it
3. Keep an eye on your favorite market and look for obvious trends.
4. Look for those trades that might satisfy your needs.

5. If you find a trade that you want to make, do it.
6. If you don't find any, go away.
7. Sleep.
8. Check your trade every morning. Try not to work through emotions and refer to our emotion-control methods. Take a big step in your business only if there is a valid reason to do so.

When dealing with other people is the main part of your career, it's incredibly important to be a fun and enjoyable person. A common explanation of the reason why many real estate agents do not last a very long time in the business is that they are difficult to work with.

Being difficult to deal with as a real estate agent is a surefire way to fail.

Advice: Always bear in mind when dealing with buyers and sellers that there are hundreds or even thousands of other agents who also might want to work with your clients. If working with an agent is difficult, finding a more likeable agent is easy enough for a buyer or a seller.

An agent who has a strong reputation with other agents is much more likely to make it in the business. Most real estate agents fail because they are impossible to work with and other agents will do their best to stop working with them.

There are hundreds of reasons why real estate markets are unique, in fact, even though they are in near proximity markets can be radically different. Another reason why a real estate agent doesn't make it in the business is because he or she can't make it through the difficult times.

When a real estate market is strong, it is normal to see the majority of the agents in the business doing well and succeeding. Since real estate is unpredictable, it is inevitable that there will eventually tough times, which is when you get to see if a real estate agent fails or not. Many real estate agents struggle because they are unable to make it in a when the market is tough.

Advice: Always prepare ahead for difficult times. Even during a strong market, growing your portfolio, your number of contacts and your overall business is extremely important. Productive agents are always researching and discovering different ways to further improve their company.

Final Thoughts

In the real estate industry, there are a lot of possibilities. But there are a lot of real estate agents who fail. It is incredibly necessary to understand why real estate agents fail, whether novice agents or experienced members.

If the number of strong real estate professionals entering the business continued to increase, this would be good for the industry. Stronger agents joining and staying in the business would mean a wonderful experience for investors, sellers, and other real estate professionals.

Fundamental #1 : Is Investing in Commercial Property the Right Strategy for You?

Investing in commercial property can be really dangerous. But these difficult transactions will help you understand if the property you might want to buy suits your financial needs and priorities and if it is the right investment strategy for you.

Cash Flow:

A cash flow plan, as the name suggests, includes knowing and managing your expectations. Before you move forward with this type of strategy, consider these questions:

If the property has a relatively low monthly cash flow, would that mean that the deal is not as good as you thought?

If the property has a greater monthly cash flow but has other uncertainties, does this mean that it's a reasonable option for my portfolio?

When answering these questions, keep in mind that the strategies for each real estate will be different. Define your expectations, control those expectations, and then assess with an impartial view if the asset can meet those expectations and thereby achieve your financial objectives.

At least, the intention of cash-flow properties is to be a more passive investment (particularly compared to a value add property).

Value Add:

A property that is called "value add," usually refers to one that needs some work done before it can either, a) reach higher monthly rent rates, or b) rent out to customers. A value add property typically needs to fulfil the following criteria:

- It needs restoration work.
- It needs maintenance.
- The property's landscape / landscaping needs enhancement.

A value-add property will have lots of moving parts, which means you'll need to rely on your local team to complete every stage effectively. You will soon realize that your cash flow will generally be lower as you add value to the property. Furthermore, after the value has been applied to the property, you will continue to see higher cash flows and a higher selling value when you eventually intend to sell the commercial property.

Holding Time:

When looking at a house, you need to decide an appropriate timeframe. For example, cash flow properties are normally ready to be rented immediately, while value-added properties need to be renovated before renting units and/or the entire house. There are some general timelines that can be anticipated for each form of business investment strategy.

- Value add properties have a holding time of 1 to 3 years.
- Buying and selling within 12 months is typical of a flipping strategy (compared to a purchase and hold strategy).
- Cash flow properties may be used to raise the money required to invest in another asset.
- Commercial properties in high appreciation areas will typically be preserved since the opportunities are higher.

Appreciation:

Remember the potential appreciation when looking at commercial properties. The following questions can help find out how long you want to hold on to the property before you decide to sell it:

- Is there a high demand for land / space to be built in the local area?
- Are more citizens (year over year) moving into this area?
- Have rent prices started to rise (or fall)?
- Are there companies flocking to the area?

These considerations will help you assess your holding time for a commercial property and provide valuable insight into the expected appreciation of the investment.

Fundamental #2 : Is Investing in if Multi-Family homes the Right Strategy for You?

Investing in multi-family property allows you to determine what sort of project you want to buy. As multi-family properties are the closest to the residential ones, most people tend to invest in it.

Cash Flow Project:

A cash flow project would usually have the following characteristics:

- High occupancy rates (ideally related to low vacancy rates, i.e. tenants usually renew year-over-year leases).
- The units are leased at or above existing rates on the market.
- Costs are minimal and/or compensated by the rents received.

Value Add Project:

A value add project would usually have the following characteristics:

- Lower occupancy rates (particularly when compared with local competitor properties).

- The units are leased below average cost on the market.
- The exterior or interior should be changed.
- High operating costs (maybe due to higher maintenance costs, higher expenses or bad management).
- Usually more difficult to handle than a cash flow property.

Hold Period Project:

For a hold time period task, first compare cash-flow to the value add potentiality of a property. The following questions will help decide whether the multi-family property suits your cash flow needs and your overall investment strategy:

- How do the rents align with existing rent prices on the market?
- How does the interior and exterior of the property (and units) compare to other houses in the area?
- Is the occupancy rate high enough to have a monthly cash flow?
- What should be done to either (a) raise monthly rents, (b) boost occupancy rates or (c) cut operating costs?

Fundamental #3 : Is Investing in Retail / Triple Net Lease the Right Strategy for You?

A triple net lease (triple-Net or NNN) refers to a leasing arrangement in which the tenant pays for all property taxes, repairs, and commercial property building insurance. The tenant also charges the "usual costs," such as rent, electricity etc. For the following reasons, investors may wish to purchase a commercial property and adopt a triple net lease:

- A less hands-on approach (usually used by retail customers).
- Returns can be smaller than other investment strategies, but this approach is more passive.
- The risk will appear to be marginally lower.
- Simple to handle (the management fee is usually lower if the property owner is involved, but most triple net leases do not have a property manager).

When you want to boost your portfolio, this technique is often applied.

Fundamental #4: Understand Commercial Property Financing

Commercial property financing is usually distinct from that for residential properties. In reality, many business opportunities allow investors to follow higher income or net worth requirements, and are often capable of making a greater financial commitment.

Interest Rates:

Interest rates for commercial assets depend on the current prime rate and it's also important to understand how banks actually borrow the money they need to give you a loan with a fixed or floating interest rate.

Prime Rate: the lowest rate that money can be borrowed commercially.

How Banks Borrow: banks get their money by borrowing at a discounted rate, lending it to you, putting an interest rate on top of that, and then making their money out of it.

Amortization:

Banks can extend the duration of amortization (AM). For example, you could have a 10-year loan with a 20-year amortization period. In the above case, the longer the AM, the less debt you owe monthly. The shorter the AM, the higher the monthly payment. As shown below, each AM time has its advantages and disadvantages:

- Longer Amortization has a lower debt payment, but it has a higher interest rate.
- Shorter Amortization has a higher debt payment, but it has a lower interest rate.

Length of Loan:

The length of the loan usually corresponds to the duration of the lease. While deciding between the funding options, it is necessary to consider both the length of the loan and the amortization period.

Triple Net Lease / Retail Financing:

Triple Net Leases and retailing financing are usually characterized by the following factors:

- The lease term must therefore be evaluated to determine both the amortization period and the loan period.
- The down payment is normally between 25 and 35%.
- The interest rate is typically lower (but depends on the down payment made, as well as the lease period).
- Banks will usually refinance the loan when the owner renews the loan. However, the interest rate can adjust at this time and be higher than the average interest rate of 5-6%.

Multi-Family Financing:

There are two types of multi-family financing opportunities:

Agency Lending: this way of financing is for properties priced at over $1 million. This kind of loan often has a 30-year amortization period and a low fixed interest rate (for a given time span).

Traditional Lending: this method of funding has different conditions for loans, it typically has an interest rate between 5-6%, and also has an amortization period of 25 years.

Single-Family Financing vs. Commercial Financing:

A single-family home financing opportunity usually follows these conditions:

1. It is amortized uniformly over the term of the loan.
2. It has a fixed interest rate for the entire loan duration.
3. The demand for single-family homes is larger, and usually a secondary market.
4. Also, it is based on a home assessment.

Commercial financing usually has the following characteristics:

1. Loan term usually coincides with the lease period.
2. This typically has a longer amortization period.
3. Generally, the fixed interest rate is for a specified period of time, and then begins a "floating" phase.
4. There is a smaller secondary market which implies higher interest rates.
5. The loan is mostly based on the property's cash flow rather than its value.

Fundamental #5: Know How To Read a Proforma

A proforma of commercial rental property is essentially a financial analysis of the asset. You will need to analyze the gross revenue, vacancy rates, as well as operational costs.

Gross Revenue:

The gross income is defined as the amount of income you will earn if the property was 100% occupied.

Vacancy:

The vacancy is generally a portion of gross revenue. While estimating vacancy (as well as expected vacancy rates), most investors can produce financial models that are 5% lower than the average occupancy rate.

Operating Costs:

The operating costs can include maintenance, utilities, property taxes and general fees. Bear in mind that you will not be paying the aforesaid operating expenses with a triple net lease property.

Generally speaking, multi-family properties are expected to see 25-40% of the operating expense gross revenue. This amount may depend on several factors, including whether the property is considered to be a cash flow or value add property. If we are talking about the last one, when evaluating operating expenses you will need to bear in mind the costs of maintenance and property updating.

Debt Service:

The debt service part of the proforma contract applies to the payment of the loan without requiring operating expenses.

Net Operating Income (o NOI) = Gross Revenue – Vacancy – Operating Expenses:

The NOI is determined as the cash you will earn before taxes are paid, but after you have paid all your operating expenses. It is necessary to remember that the debt payment is not included in the NOI.

CAP Rate:

The CAP rate is the NOI calculated as a percentage compared to what you spent for the business investment property. You can think of it as the ROI created before the existing debt is taken out.

Cash on Cash (COC):

The COC is the ROI after you've paid out the existing debt. It is crucial to think that COC is not determined on the acquisition price, but on the down payment when you buy a commercial investment property.

Internal Rate of Return (IRR):

The IRR will illustrate how your investment performs. In other words, the IRR lets you decide if your money is "increasing" adequately with your current commercial investment property or if there's another (greater) opportunity to invest that will lead you to a higher IRR.

Fundamental #6: Understand the Triple Net Lease

As mentioned earlier, several commercial real estate investors who want to take advantage of a lower risk and a passive strategy will often look for opportunities that could come with the triple net lease. It is important to remember that triple net leases are special and have different conditions that must be met before going down this path.

Absolute NNN (Triple Net):

An Absolute NNN must has the following characteristics:

- You own the building; the tenant pays all the expenses.
- The tenant must pay property taxes, repairs and insurance.
- Costs, taxes, regular rents etc. are all expressly included in the contract. In addition, it is specified how the tenant will cover the above-mentioned expenses (i.e. the tenant will "pay you back" each month for expenses in addition to the agreed monthly rent, or he will directly bill you the expenses

so that you can collect just one rent payment per month).

NN (Double Net):

In an NN, we usually follow these conditions:

- All costs are billed to the tenant with the exception of roofing, structure and parking charges.
- The costs associated with the roof can vary. Usually, in this case, the roof would be something that would last 20 to 30 years, and therefore would generally not have high costs over the duration of the contract.
- The structure will depend on when the building has been built, but also on how it has been built, which will lead to lower or higher costs for the owner.

Lease Terms:

When studying the lease terms, bear in mind the following ROI guidelines:

- If the lease term is 3 years or less, then you want an 8 % CAP or higher. That is because there typically is a higher risk associated with a lower lease term.
- If the lease term is 3 to 5 years, then you want a 7 to 8 % CAP.
- If the lease term is 5 to 10 years, then you want a 6.5 to 7 % CAP.

- If the lease term is 10 years or more, then you want a 6 % CAP.

Comps in Area (Rent and Sales):

It is important to consider the following factors when planning to invest in a commercial real estate with a triple net lease opportunity:

- Look at the rental prices for equivalent buildings in the city, as well as the typical lease terms.
- Take a look at what a similar tenant pays for rent in a similar area.
- Analyze recent local sales.
- What is the CAP on similar buildings recently sold in the area?

Grade of Tenant:

When considering a triple net lease, the tenant's grade should be evaluated. You should consider the following questions when determining the tenant's grade:

Are they creditworthy?
Can you trust the tenant?
Is there a public company that supports him or her?

In general words, the higher the tenant, the lower the CAP. Although the CAP may be lower, higher grade tenants often offer lower risks.

Fundamental #7: Understand what is the Property Management (Commercial Buildings)

In commercial real estate, the function of property management is a bit different from the one in residential real estate. Depending on the type of property, a commercial property manager will have different responsibilities. For instance, an owner usually doesn't have a property manager for triple net leases.

When the owner takes a totally passive approach, the cost of maintaining the property is usually higher.

Fundamental #8: Determine if the Investor Assistance is Needed

An industry specialist, as well as their property department, offers investor assistance to actively identify new possibilities for the real estate market.

You will gain the added value of knowing that there are local experts on the ground providing their direct input and applying their expertise to your business investments.

Leverage an advanced investor's experience when choosing your commercial property.

When Should I Use an Asset Manager?

Often, an asset manager can be used when buying a multi-tenant real estate. Asset managers can be very helpful when investors are having a very hard time trying to get a multi-tenant or multi-unit financed.

Asset managers are experts in their profession, have significant experience in the purchase and management of these asset types and can help you through the whole process. If you're a novice you can be very helpful to asset managers.

10 FAQs About Investing in Commercial Property

Remember you can always talk to your investment consultant to find out a little more about commercial properties and he or she will help you understand the best investment strategy for you.

1 – I'm interested in being a CCIM (Certified Commercial Investment Member), what can I do?

Go to CCIM.com and take at least one class of introduction, or the class 101. Such classes of education will provide a perfect introduction to the market for commercial investments.

2 – Can you get a commercial loan totally amortized for 20 – 25 years?

Yes. And if it comes from a nearby bank, it is more likely you'll get one for 25.

3 – Why does Net Operating Income o NOI not include debt service?

The short answer is that "it just doesn't." The longer answer is that borrowing is a bias, while cash isn't, which is why NOI does not provide any debt service.

4 – What is the absolute net?

Absolute net implies that all expenses are paid by the tenant. In this scenario, the gross value would be the same as the absolute net value.

5 – Would a superior grade tenant result in a little interest rate from the lender?

Yes, because the risk will be reduced to both you and your lender.

6 – Are closing costs enclosed in CAP charge NOI calculations?

The short answer is yes, given that closing costs are considered to be part of the original investment and expenses. They are therefore included within the estimation of the NOI.

8 – Who negociate a Triple Net Lease (called NNN)?

The owner is typically the one who manages an NNN. If you do want a property manager, though, you can always consider hiring one to handle the NNN.

9 – What is the true return for multi-family or retail properties?

The return depends on market demand. For instance, if there's high demand in the market, you'll typically get lower returns. That being said, the cash flow is also higher as demand is high. In other words, strategy, demand, and risk directly affect a multi-family or retail property's return.

10 – What about interest rates rising? How will that impact on my cash-flow when the rate adjusts?

In general, you will typically have rent escalations within the lease to accommodate for the increase in interest rates. This will maintain a steady cash flow as interest rates potentially rise.

Pros and cons of commercial property investment:

Planning to invest in commercial property but don't know where to get started? According to Savills NSW Metropolitan Sales Senior Executive David Hickey and Savills Sales Executive Selin Ince, here are some different factors and fundamental principles that you must take into account:

Pros

- Strong rate of return on invested capital. Commercial property typically yields an increased return on initial investment.

- Secure source of revenue.
- Structured rental changes are usually included in lease agreements.
- Longer lease periods. On average a commercial property lease is anywhere from 3 to 10 years (and sometimes more), while the average residential property leases are between six months and one year.
- The leases are usually transferable.
- The property owner is mainly responsible for the outgoings of a property, such as property taxes and water use.
- Tenants typically add value. Therefore, there is an incentive to create improvements which go hand in hand with increasing the value of your commercial building. Hence, an owner of a commercial real estate can be able to charge higher rates to later tenants.
- Larger variety of properties applied to a wide range of budgets.

Cons

- Periods without tenants can result in income loss due to vacancy.
- Difficulty paying off debt due to a reduction in revenue caused by a vacancy.

- Fit-out contributions and incentives (rent-free period).
- Wider economic conditions impacting renters' ability to pay rent (economically vulnerable).
- The biggest obstacle when entering the commercial real estate market is the upfront capital needed. Lenders may need deposits that are twice as big as those needed for residential properties.
- The money required to renew the building. Facade, roof, and facilities that meet BCA requirements.
- Change of laws regulating hours of service (for example lockout laws).
- Capital income tax and costs of transaction.

What To get In Your Commercial Investment:

Location: Finding the right location is very important, according to Mr. Wizel.

"Transportation access – national and road – can make or break a business and therefore has an important impact on renter demand," he says.

Parking is also quite significant, especially in the retail sector where buyers are required to carry purchases to their cars. Retail companies or those with a retail component also need visibility, so a main-road frontage within an existing business precinct can be vital in order to guarantee a business' success, he says.

Vacancy: Understand how many vacant stores, offices, warehouses / factories are in the area you are monitoring. When there are several vacancies, that could mean that it will be difficult to find another tenant – if you lose yours. When there are no vacancies, this is a positive business in the area is successful and you are likely to be able to easily re-lease your property again. Never buy vacancies in an area unless you're sure you can quickly find a tenant, Mr Wizel says.

The building: Seek a new, desirable and well maintained asset that needs an absolute minimum of repair work.

How To Get Into Commercial Real Estate:

Get Some Training

You need to learn as much as possible. There are specific technical organizations that teach particular skills for the commercial real estate industry. You will need these courses in order to qualify for a real estate license. So, look for a real estate program that you can take. You can do this online at your physical venue, or enroll in one. After that, work on acquiring a license to practice commercial real estate.

6 Tips to Be Successful in Real Estate business

Commercial real estate training will give you the following career options:

- General brokerage
- Property development
- Property management

General brokerage:

General commercial real estate brokerage means assisting a buyer or a seller in real estate operations, helping your clients purchasing or selling a commercial property. You may also stand in for your client in commercial real estate transaction related meetings. You are an independent contractor when following this career choice, and not an employee of any real estate firm. In addition, you get paid in terms of commissions. As a realtor, you can work for every type of commercial real estate or specialize in one of all forms. Some examples of varieties that you can invest in include corporate offices, industrial properties or retail stores.

Property development:

Other career path you can end up taking in commercial real estate is property development. It is where you are deliberately developing commercial real estate and selling it or leasing it out to get a profit. You are an actual investor. In this scenario, you're organizing funding, purchasing some land, building a commercial property there, and selling the final result. You may also choose to rent it to tenant companies or organizations. Regardless of the time and high initial capital requirements, property development is the most financially rewarding form of commercial real estate.

How To Be Prosperous In (Commercial) Real Estate:

Work with a reputable company:

The first thing you can do if you want to succeed in commercial real estate is to seek employment or work for a respectable company. One of the most significant factors in your success is the name of the company for which you are working. The company you are working with needs to have a good reputation in the commercial real estate sector. It helps a lot when you try to convince a customer to work with you.

Trusted real estate firms provide protection for clients if they invest in commercial real estate. Companies on a city, state or national level may be recognized for their good reputation. Ergo, make sure you do some research when you look for opportunities as an agent for commercial real estate. Aspire to be part of a successful and efficient company's workforce. That surely will increase the chances of success.

Pick your market wisely:

As in every other business field, the market in commercial real estate obviously matters. So, look for one that has great potential for customers and profit. The market for commercial real estate is generally stronger in the cities than in the countryside. It is because cities have higher demand, higher business activities and higher fees. Beyond that, make sure to choose cities that have a strong growth. Some cities seem to grow more than others.

Curiously, commercial real estate brokers who work in prosperous cities sign agreements and close commercial establishment deals before they're even completed. This comes about thanks to the high space demand. Therefore, target a city or regional market in order to be sure to succeed.

3 Things You need to Know About the (Commercial) Real Estate Trade You are Analyzing

How much money does it make?

What is your return on investment?

How does this investment compare to other investments?

5 Investment conditions for Commercial Real Estate:

- Income and expenses
  Each commercial immovable has both.

  Profits are made up of collected rents, lease payments, laundry revenue and even late fees.

Examples of expenses may include: insurance, taxes, utilities, repairs, landscaping, and fees for property management.

The mortgage payment is one thing that is not included in the expenses.

It is debt expense.

- Net Operating Income (NOI)
  Definition: Your income minus your expenses.

  The most important concept of these five.

  One of the most essential words of these five.

  As your net operating income goes up, it increases your cash flow and property value.

  When it goes down, also do the cash flow and the value of the property.

- Cash Flow
  Definition: Your NOI minus your mortgage payment.

- Cash-on-cash return
  How fast is your money moving?

  If you get your money back in 1 year, it is 100% cash-on-cash return

  If you get your money back in 2 years, it is 50% cash-on-cash return

- Capitalization Rate
  "Cap Rate" is NOI divided by the sales price.

  If you are paying all the cash for your investment, what's the return on that investment?

  A high cap rate property should be located in a neighborhood of low to moderate income.

  The higher you go, the higher the risk, the higher the possible return but the lower the value.

  There is a low cap rate in a wealthier neighborhood.

  Higher cap rates mean lower risk but also lower return and higher sale price.

Rules for These Five Key Terms (10:06):

- Always determine each of these terms, do not make an offer until you do so
- The income you need must be greater than the expenses.
- The NOI must be greater than the mortgage payments.
- The cash-flow have to be be positive.
- The cash-on-cash return has to be approximately equivalent to 10%.
- Cap rate must be approximately equivalent to 8%.

Whether you are an entrepreneur, broker, mortgage lender, solar installer, project manager or carpenter, it's always an important part of the game to measure and understand commercial properties and identify profitable opportunities.

Commercial Property Analysis

It takes you a bit of preliminary research to identify potential value assets, but this investigation is just that — preliminary.

Analyzing property is where the real work begins. It is where real data on properties and their owners can be used to make your speculation a certainty. Numbers, narratives, indications and assurance are the four things nearly all commercial real estate professionals should be searching for in their property evaluation.

Numbers are the gritty information of a property — the associated years, dates, costs, and measurements.

Narratives are the stories behind a property and its history. Every property has histories of sales, debt, and ownership that can influence how an investor, lender, or service provider is dealing with the property at the current moment.

Indications are signals which point to the intentions or possible actions of a property owner. They are the statistics and insights that prove the will or willingness of an owner to sell, refinance, rebuild, repair, etc.

Essentially, assurance is confirmation that a property is worth considering. Assurance is based on finding the correct numbers, narratives and property-linked indications.

Now that you know exactly what you are looking for, let's talk about how to find opportunities.

Building and Lot Analysis

First and foremost, you should evaluate a commercial building and the lot to see whether it is up to date with your criteria for investment, leasing or service. Mostly, you get numbers with a bit of history here.

The lot size, building size, building age, and zoning can be examined. See lot square footage and acreage, as well as square footage of buildings, number of units, number of buildings, number of stories and floor area.

Using Google's interactive map view, building service providers such as roofers, solar installers, and landscapers can use "Reonomy" to evaluate a building's physical structure and features, its roof, and its surrounding land.

To examine street-level and aerial shots of your target properties simply combine your experience with the map view on any property profile page.

Investment Analysis

By analyzing a property's sales history and its owner's preferences, you can see if a property represents a potential investment opportunity.

Try searching a property. In this scenario, an investor may search on a particular place for properties of a specific asset type that have not been sold in the last ten years. This distinguishes instantly those who are more likely to sell, and weeds out those who are not.

You can click on the profile page of any individual property from your results list, and visit the "Sales" section.

Ask any good real estate agent about the benefits of investing in commercial property, and you are likely to provoke a monolog about how these properties are better than residential properties. Commercial property owners enjoy the extra cash flow, the fairly open playing field, the plentiful demand for good, the affordable property managers and the wider payoff.

But how do you recognize the best properties? And what helps distinguish great deals from scams?

As with most real estate properties, success begins with a good plan. Here's one to help you determine a great deal for commercial property.

Learn What the Insiders Know

Learn to think like a professional, to be a player in commercial real estate. For instance, know that a commercial property is valued differently from a residential property. Commercial property income is directly linked to its usable lot size. But residential homes are working differently. You'll can see a wider cash flow with commercial property. The reason for this is simple: you will receive more revenue on multi-family residential buildings, for example, than on a single-family home. You also need to know that commercial property contracts are longer than the ones for single-family homes. That opens up the opportunity for more cash flow. Finally, if you're in a tighter credit environment, make sure you have cash in your hands. Lenders of commercial property like to see at least 30% down before they give a loan.

Map Out a Plan of Action

In a commercial real estate transaction setting conditions is a top priority. For instance, ask yourself how much you can pay for mortgages, and then shop around and get a sense of how much you will probably have to spend. The use of tools such as mortgage calculators can help you create accurate estimations of your home's overall cost.

Other important questions you have to ask yourself include: How much do you expect the deal to make? Who are the main players? How many tenants are on board and are still paying rent? How much rental space do you need?

Learn to Recognize a Good Deal

True real estate professionals know a good deal whenever they see one. What is their secret? Firstly, they have an exit strategy: the best deals are those from which you know you can walk away. It helps to have a clear, landowner's perspective – constantly finding damage that needs to be repaired, knowing how to manage risk, and making sure the property satisfies your goals and objectives.

Look for Motivated Sellers:

Like any business, clients power real estate. Your goal is to find them – especially those who are eager and willing to sell below market price. The fact is, nothing occurs or even makes little difference in real estate until you find a deal that is usually followed by a motivated seller. This is someone who has an urgent reason to sell below market price.

Discover the Fine Art of Neighborhood "Farming":

A great way to evaluate a commercial property is to study its neighborhood by going to open houses, talking to other nearby owners, and trying to look for vacant positions.

Use a "Three-Pronged" Approach to Evaluate Properties:

Seek great deals and be able to adapt. Use the web, read the ads online and consider hiring someone to find the best properties for you. Real estate bird dogs, in exchange for a referral fee, can help you discover valuable investment leads.

The Bottom Line:

Finding and assessing real estate is not just about farming neighborhoods, getting great prices, or using smoke signals to get sellers to you. At heart, there's a basic human need for communication. It is all about building relationships and interacting with property owners so they feel at ease talking about the great deals – and doing business with you.

Real estate is a market for people. Although working with clients can offer a lot of benefits, there are also some complications. Often a real estate agent is going to be in a position where he or she has to deal with a challenging customer who is unreasonable, challenging, or just plain annoying. However, it is only by succeeding in dealing with these clients that the agent can gain the title of a real professional.

Every single customer is different. Your prospects are people with different personality traits, so a successful real estate agent needs to be able to recognize these types of personalities. Of course, it's impossible to satisfy everyone, but if you know the types of people you're working with, you'll be prepared to deal with any major problem and have satisfied customers. Here are six types of tough real estate clients and a few tricks for realtors on how to handle them:

Types of Negative Clients

Know It All: These clients believe they know more about the real estate market than you do and are very dismissive of your advice, sure that they know what they are doing. Ultimately, what they perceive as "knowledge" can impede you doing your job.

The Client Negative: Gloomy, pessimistic and demotivating. Either with what you show them, or with your advice on how to sell their house, they'll find something wrong with just about everything. They may be irrational, and hard to reach an agreement with.

People Pleaser: In comparison to the negative client, pleaser people are polite and hate to say anything bad. These clients always say " yes, "but they're poor to deliver.

The Do-Nothing: these clients don't say anything or give feedback. Typically, their first answer to your requests is "I don't know”. Since they're unsure, they may say one thing on the call, but they'll have a different opinion afterwards. This can become a barrier to communication and can discourage you from finding their dream home.

Clients Rant-and-Rave: Noisy, bossy, and over-react about anything. For example, they could say, "Are you crazy? How are you going to list my house at such a low price?”. These characteristics could make a conflict between you and your client and make your job a bit complicated.

The Rude Client: This client thinks that his or her needs always come first, and behaves like you don't have any other customers. They will keep following-up via messages, emails, and voicemails before you have even had the chance to evaluate the situation or to draw up a list of homes to visit.

CHAPTER 4: HOW TO FIND REAL ESTATE PARTNERSHIPS: A GUIDE TO OWNER FINANCING

Asking a seller to help you purchase your home or commercial real estate is not commonly accepted by most homeowners or even their listing agents. Nevertheless, owner financing is unquestionably a viable option for a seller whose property is not selling or for a buyer who is having trouble with the traditional lender guidelines.

What's Owner Financing?

Owner (or seller) Financing means that the current owner puts up some or all of the money required to buy a property: instead of taking out a mortgage from a commercial lender, the buyer borrows the money from the seller. Under this way, buyers can finance a transaction completely, or have a loan from the seller and another from the bank.

The buyer and seller settle on an interest rate, monthly payment, money amount, schedule, and other lending information. The buyer then gives the seller a commitment note which agrees to these terms. The promissory note is usually deposited in the public records, and thus both parties are assured.

It doesn't matter if the property has an existing mortgage on it, but due to an alienation clause the lender of the homeowner may accelerate the loan upon sale. Generally, the lender holds the title to the house until the borrower has completely repaid the loan.

Different kinds of Owner Financing

Sellers and buyers are free to discuss the terms of owner financing, subject to state-specific usury laws and other local regulations: for example, some state laws ban balloon payments.

Although not needed, many sellers expect the buyer to make some kind of down-payment on the property. Their logic is close to that of any mortgage lender: they believe buyers with any equity in a house are less likely to default on the payments and let it go into foreclosure.

Owner financing can take several forms. Some variations include the following:

Land Contracts

Land contracts do not transfer the full legal title of the property to the buyer, but they give them an equitable title. For a certain time, the buyer must make payments to the seller. The buyer collects the deed after final payment or a refinancing.

Mortgages

Sellers can carry the mortgage for the entire purchase price balance — less the down payment, which could include an underlying loan. This type of financing is called an all-inclusive mortgage or trust deed, also famous as a wrap-around mortgage too. The seller gets an interest override on the underlying loan. A seller can also hold a junior mortgage, in which case the buyer would take title or receive a new first mortgage, relative to the current loan. The buyer receives a deed and gives the seller a second mortgage for the purchase price difference, minus the down payment and the first portion of the mortgage.

Lease-purchase Agreements

A lease-purchase agreement, also known as rent to own, means the seller is leasing the property to the buyer, giving them an equitable title to it. Upon fulfillment of the lease-purchase agreement, the buyer receives the full title and generally obtains a loan to pay the seller, after receiving credit for all or part of the rental payments towards the original cost.

Owner-Financing Benefits for Buyers

Buyers who opt for owner financing can enjoy several advantages:

Little or No Qualifying

The seller's definition of buyer requirements is usually less strict and more flexible than the qualifications decided by traditional lenders.

Tailored Financing

Unlike traditional loans, sellers and buyers can pick from a number of options for loan repayment, such as interest-only, fixed-rate amortization, less-than-interest, or a balloon payment —if the state allows it—or even a combination of these. Interest rates for the term of the loan can adjust periodically or remain at one rate.

Down Payment Flexibility

Down payments are negotiable. When a seller needs a greater down payment than the buyer possesses, sellers may also require buyers to make periodic lump-sum payments towards a down payment.

Lower Closing Costs

There is no loan or discount points without an institutional lender, and no origination fees, processing fees, administration fees, or any of the other various miscellaneous fees that lenders frequently charge, which also saves money on buyer closing costs.

Faster Possession

Since buyers and sellers aren't waiting for a lender to process the financing, buyers can close more quickly and get ownership of the property sooner than with a conventional loan.

Owner-Financing Benefits for Sellers

When talking about owner financing situations, a number of advantages also emerge for sellers:

Monthly Income

Payments from a buyer increase the monthly cash flow of the seller resulting in an expendable income.

Higher Sales Price

Because the seller is offering the financing, they may be able to request the full list price, or higher.

Higher Interest Rate

The owner-financed loan can bring a higher interest rate than a seller would receive on a money market account or other forms of low-risk investment.

Tax Breaks

The seller might pay less tax on an installment sale, declaring only the revenues earned in each calendar year.

Quicker Sale

Offering owner financing is one way to stand out from the inventory sea, attracting a different set of customers and selling properties that would otherwise be hard to sell.

Advantageous as it can be, owner financing is very complex. Neither buyer nor seller should rely exclusively on their respective real estate agents but should instead hire real estate lawyers to assist them in negotiating the transaction, ensuring that their arrangement conforms to all state laws, covers any risk and safeguards all parties equally.

ADVANTAGES OF HAVING A PARTNER: HOW TO FIND REAL ESTATE PARTNERSHIP

A substantial portion of new entrepreneurs who consider entering the real estate industry tend to fear the unknown. Going alone in the industry can be frightening and often discourages anyone from making a valid investment decision. Learning how to find an investment partner in real estate can be a lucrative skill for investors of any level.

Even the brightest and most successful real estate investors learn something new every day. It's almost impossible to know every aspect of an investment and how best to manage it without any help. Some advantages of having a partner include:

1. More Experience
2. Task Delegation

3. Additional Funds
4. Divided Risks
5. New Contacts

Someone who is looking for a real estate partner will benefit from the process when working with the right people. It is common for a novice to look for a partner with more experience. When it comes to making additional investments in homes for sale, partners are also great at generating more funds. This give a way to divide the hazard between multiple groups. One last benefit of establishing a real estate collaboration is the extra connections that can be acquired. Many people have vast lists of acquaintances, business partners, and brokers in the housing industry that are very useful.

Where to find a partner

Finding someone to work with in just about every major U.S. city is relatively easy. Some real estate agents go into business with investors in order to earn an additional living apart from their day full time job. Partnering with a professional who attends a real estate investment club in a local town can open more doors. Placing an advertisement requesting a partner's assistance on a reputable website for the housing industry can produce some good prospects in general.

Business formation for Real Estate

It is becoming more ordinary between investors to go into written agreement together and make an LLC or other type of accord. While taxation is important to understand, acknowledging the legalities of working together and the state and federal laws pertaining to a real estate business is also important. It is also better to use the services of an attorney to establish a working arrangement with another party before signing any document. Ensuring that an exit strategy is in place will help break the relationship in the event that it does not work as expected. A division of held property and return on investment should be clearly defined. Having a positive mindset, completing everyday tasks, and working towards the objectives of the partnership can create a healthy atmosphere for any investor.

THE ALTERNATIVE TO FIND PARTNERSHIPS? BE A SELF-MADE INVESTOR

Think about the most important investors in history. Most of them are self-made investors. Who is a self-made businessman? He is a person who has very interesting ideas, an extensive background in the field, and who, in most cases, bets on everything he has, and has made some clever choices in order to achieve his or her goals. Normally, this kind of person has a very detailed plan and follows it slavishly.

If you really have the "power" to do it, just do it.

Each of these people have some characteristics in common, some key concepts for investment that helped make them billionaires. Along with every great secret in life, this one is hidden in plain sight. In fact, these self-made billionaire investors...

1. Don't diversify

Consider what your main source of wealth generation possibly is: your career. You have probably not diversified into your profession at all. Even if you've tried a lot of different careers, you never did a few at once. And, even if you're doing more than one job, it's highly likely that you're spending the vast majority of your time on just one of them, and that only one provides the vast majority of your earnings.

Why should investing be any different?

2. Avoid risk

If you want to be a good investor you must always quantify all the risks and make transparent business plans. You will quickly be able to plan your work and your future in business and real estate investments. Keep yourself informed, and prepare to invest after studying.

3. Don't care about what anyone else thinks

Lots of people get a feel for where a market is going. But they never talk about what they are buying or selling. They just do it.

Think for yourself, avoid risk, and do not try to diversify into a bunch of investments that you don't understand.

CHAPTER 5: TAX ADVANTAGES OF COMMERCIAL REAL ESTATE

Unlike bonds, stocks, and other financial products, the commercial real estate business is known for the various tax benefits that real estate investors can take advantage of. These benefits can make a huge difference in income, especially in the long run. However, to take advantage of the tax benefits of commercial real estate, you need to know what they are and how they work. The most common forms of reduction of tax accounts for investors can be:

1. Qualified Business Income (QBI) Deductions
2. Interest Expenses Tax Deduction
3. Depreciation Deduction for income tax
4. 1031 Exchanges for Capital Gains Tax Deferral
5. Using Real Estate Taxes Losses to Your Advantage
6. Tax Benefits of Commercial Real Estate vs IRAs for Retirement
7. Non-Mortgage Tax Deduction
8. Reduced Tax Burdens for Beneficiaries
9. Opportunity Zones

Qualified Business Income (QBI) Deductions:

Deduction of Qualified Business Income (QBI) is another complex deduction that commercial real estate investors can make on income taxes. The QBI exemption covers income from passive sources and allows eligible individuals to deduct 20% of eligible income. However, it is somewhat difficult to determine how much you can use.

Some restrictions include 50% of the W-2 payment or, 25% of the W-2 payment, with 2.5% of the depreciated site of the property in question. Most of the time, the second calculation is used, and most CRE investments are made by some employees of the SPE if any. It should also be noted that capital gains from the sale of commercial assets are not considered QBI exempt revenues.

Interest Expenses Tax Deduction:

Investors can depreciate more quickly in the form of debt amortization, but a series of cost-sharing analyses can help speed up depreciation. In fact, the new provisions of the 2017 Employment and Cuts Act may exempt some investors from the first year of ownership depreciation up to 100% of the value of the asset.

Depreciation Deduction for income tax:

As with other physical assets, commercial real estate depletes over time. This allows investors to deduct a certain amount from income tax each year. The IRS now allows homeowners to reduce homes for 27.5 years and commercial buildings for 39 years. For example, if an investor buys $ 5 million in office space, he may receive $ 128,000 in depreciation annually. Depreciation is good for investors, but there is much that an investor can do to cover significant depreciation in a short period of time. In many situations, investors can request a depreciation analysis from an engineering firm that identifies different parts of an asset in as little as five or ten years. For example, in the example above (for example, roofs and electrical components), a $ 1 million asset could be depreciated over ten years, and the owner could consider reducing that portion of the asset by $ 100,000. This results in a $ 202,000 reduction per year for the first ten years and $ 102,000 per year for the remaining 29 years. Cost-sharing studies can be used for many family and business characteristics, but are typically used for multiple family ones.

Depreciation: badly needed

Although depreciation has lots of benefits, the IRS can recover if investors sell assets in the form of depreciation recovery. A depreciation withdrawal is triggered when an investor sells an asset over an adjusted cost basis that is less than the asset's original cost depreciation deduction. For example, if an investor sells beyond $ 4 million after ten years (the original price is estimated to be $ 5million, then depreciation is $ 1 million), depreciation will begin to be collected. For this reason, investors must pay the regular income tax rate on the sale price of the property, rather than lower the capital gains tax rate.

Interest Expense Tax Deductions:

An important tax benefit of commercial real estate is that you can deduct interest payable on commercial mortgages from federal mortgage tax. For example, if a commercial real estate lender pays $ 10,000 per month for mortgage payments and $ 2000 of that interest, the mortgage interest is deductible at around $ 24,000 that year. This is particularly relevant if the borrower has access to high-interest rate loans, such as construction loans.

The LIHTC, HTC, and NMTC Programs:

Together with the Opportunity Zone plan, the federal government's LIHTC (Low-Income Home Tax Credit) program allows investors with low-income, qualified assets to be exempt from federal income tax. In some cases, you can link your LIHTC program to an opportunity zone program to increase your revenue. Other widely used tax credit schemes include the Historic Tax Credit (HDC) scheme and credit loan plans that provide tax credits based on a percentage of eligible costs used for rehabilitation of historic commercial buildings. In general, these tax credits are competitive and are typically used by companies and funds, rather than individual investors.

In this regard, it is important that commercial real estate investors consult with experienced tax professionals to better understand how each of these tax incentives works.

Real estate taxes are very complex, and a great deal of work on products and documentation can save more money in the long run.

1031 Exchanges for Capital Gains Tax Deferral:

The 1031 Exchange is another very useful method that can be used to advantage commercial real estate investors. The 1031 transaction allows commercial real estate investors to postpone the payment of capital gains tax to the IRS and exchange assets for another "similar" commercial real estate within a certain period of time. A similar property must be at least as good as the initial property and must not be a detached house used as the owner's private residence. However, the types of real estate to be traded need not be the same. For example, a multipurpose retail apartment/property can be exchanged for a mall. However, the 1031 exchange does not allow investors to unnecessarily postpone capital gains. When a new real estate is sold, investors have to pay all taxes. However, nothing prevents investors from selling real estate and engaging in another exchange in 1031.

Using Real Estate Taxes Losses to Your Advantage:

In general, there are three different classifications of taxpayers from commercial real estate to rental losses. Commercial real estate investors below $ 100,000 per year: these people can lose an income of up to $ 25,000. For example, if an investor makes $ 90,000 a year and loses more than $ 25,000 a year, his taxable income for that year may be reduced to $ 65,000. Anyone who earns up to $ 100,000 and up to $ 150,000 can receive a deductible, but not as much as those who earn less than $ 100,000. If a commercial real estate investor earns $ 150,000 or more per year, there is no deduction relating to the loss of commercial real estate.

Tax Benefits of Commercial Real Estate vs IRAs for Retirement:

Unlike IRAs, which are taxed at the investor's normal personal tax rate when the fund is withdrawn, when lenders sell commercial properties they typically pay lower capital gains tax than the personal income tax, at least for most investors. Note, however, that this does not apply to the Roth IRA.

Non-Mortgage Tax Deduction:

Corporate and multi-family real estate investors, in addition to mortgage interest expenses, can deduct income tax from property repairs, maintenance, certain asset management costs and many operating expenses. This includes hotel expenses, round-trip costs for rental properties, and 50% of drinks and foods. Investors can also deduct property investments for expenses related to seminars, conferences, and other similar educational events. However, general improvements to the property such as renovation and new furniture, in general, cannot be considered exempt for the year in which they occur.

Commercial Real Estate Experts:

If you are considered a commercial real estate professional appointed by the IRS, there is no limit to the number of real estate losses you can receive in a year. To qualify, a person must work at least 750 hours per year in positions related to real estate, such as real estate managers, brokers, agents and investors. In addition, they usually have to work in this position longer than any other job. Due to the tax advantages of being a real estate professional, some investors have decided to abandon their full-time employments to pursue wealth management and full-time investments.

Reduced Tax Burdens for Beneficiaries:

Commercial property owners not only have tax credits but also have significant tax advantages for their heirs. For example, if an investor buys commercial property for $ 3 million and the value rises to $ 4.5 million before the investor dies, the investor's beneficiaries will have $ 1.5 million in total assets instead of $ 4.5 million. All you have to do is pay taxes. This can save hundreds of thousands of dollars.

Opportunity Zones:

The Opportunity Zone program was created under the 2017 Tax Reduction and Employment Act and is designed to promote investment in low-income communities across the United States. Until 31 December, qualified capital gains will be postponed, allowing their fund to invest in specially funded vehicles, its assets will be at least 90%, commercial real estate and qualified features will be 8700. In addition, investors can reduce their capital gains tax base by 10% if they hold investments for at least five years by 31 December 2026. Investors can reduce their underlying taxable capital gains by an additional 5% when having invested for at least seven years.

CHAPTER 6 : HOW TO RAISE CAPITAL

Do you know how real estate finance works? Investing in real estate has become the definition of "American dream". Real estate is currently firing, and there is no reason why people cannot participate in this activity. The difficulties in order to enter in the field are minimal; all you need is the right amount of interest, a little due diligence and the best real estate education.

The most important thing in real estate is capital. Investing in real estate requires capital, but it is not essential that this capital is yours. In fact, you don't have to invest your own money. It is entirely possible to invest in real estate using other people's money or thanks to what I call OPM. If at the beginning the money is not yours, you must develop strategies in order to attract others interested in financing your real estate activities. You should try to sell yourself to every investor.

Indeed, venture capitalists are willing and able to lend money to those who make some profit. If you choose to accept it, your goal is to make them aware of the value of the investment. You must convince venture capital investors that you are worth their time and money. You need to learn what venture capital investors want from the right investors.

A company is fundamental in the development and financing of larger real estate projects.

Financial methods to invest in four different ways of real estate:

Real estate initiatives can require more money than anything else. It could be argued that fundraising for real estate transactions is very important and essential. Therefore, investors need to know the most efficient ways not only to get the right funds but also to make them easily accessible. It is not difficult to learn how to raise capital. Many lenders are waiting for reputable debtors to pay. Investors need to know where to look.

Retirement accounts:

It is possible to invest in real estate real estate using a personal retirement account (IRA). Through the Internal Revenue Service (IRS), eligible account holders can send their savings to property investments. Of course, an account holder must have a guardian who wants the account owner to manage his or her assets.

Investors can use the funds in their retirement accounts to buy real estate while their accounts are self-managed. All profits made must be returned to the original account. However, profits may increase deferred taxes. Thus, investors may not be able to spend money immediately, but the resulting tax relief will increase their profitability.

Private placement notes:

Private employment tips are still the best source of funding. Private employment tips are similar to private offers. However, private placements, in particular, offer to real estate developers the opportunity to raise capital by selling securities to other investors.

Individuals and individual payers:

Hard money lenders are semi-institutionalized lenders that are generally allowed to lend to those in need. Private lenders, on the other hand, tend to access and invest in capital. There are subtle differences between these two types of lenders, but they are still the most popular sources of funding.

As their name implies, private and private money lenders are not subject to the same "bureaucracy" because they are not affiliated with institutional banks. On the contrary, these lenders tend to work alone and usually struggle to lend to those in need. These lenders can offer short-term, high-interest loans to investors primarily based on significant ownership. Private and hard currency lenders make decisions based on the loan, depending on whether the property in question is a valuable investment. This means that investors do not need to have the right credit score to get approval, but they need to have a good work ethic.

In exchange for giving access to their capital, most private and cash lenders require about 12-15% interest and some additional points (prepayment interest). Although their interest rates are much higher (almost three times) than traditional banks, it is understandable that these lenders can give to investors an immediate access to capital. On the other hand, it can take a month or two for a bank to provide for funds. You may lose many opportunities before getting money from a bank. Therefore, the pace of execution provided by private and private lending institutions has made funding for real estate transactions much easier.

Even if it is not traditionally considered as a source of funding, the overall practice has gained a reputation by allocating relatively quick funding to interested investors. Most importantly, you do not even need initial funding to use the strategic allocation of contracts. It is entirely possible to make money in just a few hours without using the funds of a fully executed investor. Even if they are not a traditional source of funding, wholesale sales can certainly help investors interested in financing real estate transactions.

How to Protect Real Estate Investment Capital:

To raise money for a real estate transaction, you need to know where investors can find resources. Once you know where to get it, you need to know how to save money. As a result, investors need to learn where to find the money they need. As I said, countless lenders are waiting to lend to today's investors. However, it is responsibility of the investor to prove that he or she is worth the investment.

Take a look at some of the most important aspects that venture capitalists and private money lenders look for when they want to raise money for a real estate venture:

- Show your experience.
- Define group structure.
- Explain the benefits of opportunities.
- Experiential experience.

The experience of establishing credibility plays an important role in raising funds for real estate investing.

Given this, how can new investors compensate for inexperience? Even the most successful investors started from the bottom. No one was born having years of experience. Therefore, new investors are encouraged to compensate for their lack of experience in knowledge and attention to detail. You may be surprised at how much less diligence and motivation it takes. At this point, you need to have confidence. Do not put your experience or lack thereof at the center of any particular deal.

In fact, venture capitalists and money lenders want to work with people who feel comfortable giving money.

Group structure:

The best investors know that real estate is a talent business. All transactions require the cooperation of at least two parties. However, if you want to learn how to raise money for a real estate venture, you need to work well with others, especially with your own team. Private lenders focus on trust with the team and they have a good reason for that. A talented team with the right leaders can do almost anything. But what makes a team talented? Before you decide to provide the funds needed to finance the transaction, what will the borrower look for in your group? Learning how to raise money for a real estate venture begins with a group setting. Before you consider making money, make sure your team has the following qualities:

Dedication: A little more important to an entrepreneur than a team, and less important to a team. Without commitment, even the most talented real estate teams can collapse. As an investor, it is in your greatest interest to outlaw obligations from those who choose to work together.

Passion: The best teams show a great passion. It should be noted. However, that interest gradually diminishes. To lead a passionate team, you must be interested in your future endeavors. Let people understand how excited you are about the future day of your organization. Make sure people are interested in the idea of working with you. At least they will know that your heart is in the right place.

Teamwork: Teamwork, sometimes called "chemistry", is a force that leads a team to be able to collaborate in a unique way, and venture capitalists are well aware of that power. Demonstrate to investors that you can work well with different investors.

Flexibility: Flexible entrepreneurs are inherently strict. Serious investors are not adaptive and are prone to problems. Flexibility, in that way, gives investors the opportunity to think down-to-earth. All the most important entrepreneurs of our time have demonstrated their ability to be flexible. No one can mitigate risk better than the ability to adapt to changing conditions.

Diligence: Although not entirely different from curiosity, perseverance praises it. Some say that firmness alone is what separates adults from big investors. No verdict has been released yet, but intrinsic team perseverance can certainly help persuade others to work for you.

Knowledge: Knowledge is power, more than any other aspect of this list. This is your most important asset. Knowledge recognizes if everything is working properly. One of the most important attributes that a group can boast of is real estate education.

"Cosmopolitan": In my opinion, if you can't coach, you are ignorant. Smart men don't know everything. Coaching helps a lot to gain the confidence of others. Not only will you learn, but if you want to admit that you are wrong, you will open up a whole new way of working with others.

Opportunity:

Also, one of the best ways to generate money for a real estate venture is to make sure lenders value their time. There is nothing better than convincing a lender to pay you more quickly. Remember that you are the one raising money for real estate investing. It's up to you to see if they want to give you credit. The house you are going to invest in has to do most of the work. Nonetheless, run the numbers yourself and give the lender a reason not to spend the money elsewhere.

At this point, you will want to express your intentions in advance. Tell us how much you are looking for and what potential benefits your investment in your business will bring. It is up to you to explain all the transactions.

Successful investments in real estate require less risk, and private lenders are no exception. They are not professionals who throw money away. They want to make sure you can deliver them.

Fundraising for real estate investing is an essential step for all real estate investors. The property in question is the big reason why people pay, but it's only a small part of the equation. Lenders want to be comfortable with the people who pay them. In this regard, the most successful lenders have learned how to identify the best investors. A person who makes more money and returns interest. Exercise these characteristics every day if you want to be an investor's lender. In other words, a proven source of income. So, you will definitely be overwhelmed by all these options on how to finance real estate development.

1. Financial Methods for Real Estate Development: Traditional Bank Finance

   There is good news if you are considering traditional bank lending. For the first time in nearly three years, banks have relaxed the standards for commercial real estate loans. This is an incentive to renew traditional bank loans. In fact, America's five largest banks have experienced the worst quarter in the last 20 years. Home loan inflows were down to $ 87 billion in the first quarter of 2018, up from $ 110 billion in the previous quarter. The lender evaluates the applicant's assets, credit history, and debt-to-income ratio by analyzing several documents:

   Bank Statement: Determines if there are balance fees that can last for several months in the event of an emergency.

Credit history: Evaluates the risk of exposure to deficiencies such as previous foreclosures.

Latest Payslips: Measures your current earnings. Applicants who are self-employed or have other sources of income can provide evidence using forms such as Form 1099 or Direct Deposit.

Form W-2 and Tax Revenue: Ensure consistency between annual income and reported income on payroll and identify changes in income.

All the way: Minimum credit, excellent credit score, good and stable income, and patience to handle the paperwork.

If you fulfil all these requirements and pay low fees (about 20-25% of the purchase price), you will definitely benefit from lower interest rate bank loans.

2. Financial System for Real Estate Development: Loan from Credit Union

As the bank's mortgage market share shrank, its share increased from 8% in Q2 2016 to 10% in Q2 2017. Credit unions, like banks, offer clear and fair options. One of the key features that differentiate banks from credit unions is customer service. Banks have lower customer satisfaction rates than credit unions, ranking 82 out of 100 in the 2017 Customer Satisfaction Report. Because banks usually have more branches and technological advancements, it says. There can be many contacts for credit union members. However, this is a special issue for loan applicants due to additional membership requirements.

Two important attractions that give credit unions an advantage over banks are:

- Tax-exempt for non-profits.
- Reducing fees despite higher interest rates than banks.

Also, unlike non-deposit lenders, a provider can access multiple services like;

- Home assets line of credit
- Home equity loans.
- Mortgage.

In addition to maintaining these accounts, we establish relationships with financial institutions and record financial information. Permanent prior approval for secondary funding may be obtained.

3. Financing for Real Estate Development: Real Estate Peer-to-Peer Lending

The global peer-to-peer lending market is expected to steadily increase from $ 26,064 million in 2015 to $ 460,312 million by 2022.

The central market matches lenders (individuals and investors) with borrowers through online services. Unlike banks, the overhead costs (staff, other business lines, branch networks) are very low, which means that B2B loans are surprisingly low. Of course, you need a good credit score, but you can still get a lower than perfect score.

Evaluate these features when analyzing the best peer-to-peer lending platform.

- Required prepaid appearance fee.
- Data protection like financial institutions.
- Information Privacy Policy on Personal Information.

4. How to Raise Capital for Real Estate Growth: Buy real estate with FHA loans

If you decide to borrow from a traditional bank with more limited requirements, you can get a loan from the Federal Housing Administration (FHA). Here, a first-time homebuyer benefits from lower rates. The FHA guarantees such loans, so lenders offer generous terms. Borrowers can benefit from FHA loan protection not found in traditional mortgages. But it's still based on your credit history. A minimum of 580 FICO score is required to qualify for a 3.5% lower fee. A lower credit score means about 10% higher payment costs. If you use debt to set up multiple family properties, you can live in one unit and rent the other.

5. Financing System for Real Estate Development: Hard Money Loan

In the second quarter of 2018, 48,768 condominium and single-family homes fell in the United States (the fall is a two-time-traded home between sellers and unrelated buyers within 12 months). 38.6% of those homes were purchased with home financing.

Traditional bank loans often take time to get approved and are based on the borrower's credit score. Fortunately, hard cash loans are secured by the real estate you buy. It speeds up approval without extensive requirements. However, you are more likely to pay in advance for a loan process (a smaller price you have to pay for a loan that is 100% of the home purchase price). Interest rates are in general higher than conventional banking company loans.

CHAPTER 7: HOW TO GET THE BEST FROM RENTING AND PASSIVE INCOME

Making money from daytime work will add value to your network. You may have heard of passive income. Renting real estate is the norm. But before you first step in, there are some things you should learn about real estate rentals as a source of passive income. Let's break them down.

How to get passive income from rental properties:

First, get a direct record of passive income. Passive income is income derived from sources that require minimal effort. A few examples are stock and bond investments or returns on real estate. In general, passive income is the best: it can help to raise retirement benefits, encourage early retirement or meet wealth-building goals more quickly. There are many ways to invest in real estate right now, but let's talk about the popular ones, especially for what concerns rent and passive income. Once you start and run a rental, rental properties are a major source of passive income. It isn't completely passive, as the startup requires some effort (especially if you need to refresh the startup to plan for the rental). However, you can provide monthly income without participating daily and directly

How:

If you're buying a property for rent and you're new to rental games, find a reasonable, stable midway point. Borrowing hundreds of thousands of dollars to "invest" in real estate is never a good idea! If possible, buy one with 70% off the current market value. I try to invest as much as possible and make money.

Where to buy:

In general, good schools and houses in renowned areas are rated higher than low-priced properties (such as apartments and condominiums). Search for properties in strong areas where the prices of homes have increased over the years. Responsible tenants should not damage the place or become unpredictable when payments are made. Properties close to public transportation and major highways are generally popular with leasing companies. Beware of big corporations moving to areas of town and opening offices and other factories. It is not desirable to have your first rental in a place where you cannot regularly check the status of your property. If so, the property has to be handled by someone else (we will tell you more about that later). However, in some circumstances it can be rewarding if you choose a city with a good rental market and a fair growth in employment.

What to buy:

You must decide what to buy and what to rent. Do you need an apartment that will last for a long time? Or do you want a house you intend to sell in a couple of years to make a profit? Foreclosure is a great way to buy property straight away. Nonetheless, you should generally avoid wasting money when planning on renting a place. All you need is something that is appealing and almost ready. If you don't plan to manage the property yourself, almost everything from rentals to repairs, complaints and evictions will be handled by a real estate agent. You pay the agent a commission, so you'll be less frustrated if you're too busy to deal with these things.

Always talk to your real estate agent about how much to rent. Don’t expect too much. The monthly rent should, in fact, be adequate for maintenance, HOA fees, homeowner’s insurance, and so on. Otherwise, you don't get paid!

Happy tenants are simple tenants:

If you are managing the location yourself, do the right thing and contact your tenant every month to make sure he is not bothered. Generally, simple mails work. Do not call or visit every week without notice. You need to respect his or her privacy, but feel free to contact if you have any issues. Before renting, make sure hot water and the air conditioning system are working properly.

When to invest in rental properties:

Before thinking about buying a place to rent, there should be no debt. You need a fully funded emergency fund which will cover 3-6 months of expenses.

Getting an emergency fund is really necessary when you're a landlord for unforeseen events like repairs, unpaid rent, vacancy times, etc. As I have said, cash can be used to fund investments in real estate. This can be maintained after investing 15% of your monthly income in retirement accounts such as 401 (k) and IRA.

Get help from an expert:

If you are wondering if a rental investment is right for you and you don't know where to invest, a good real estate agent's help is required. If you are all alone, the decision to make is huge, and these people are experts who can help you buy and sell thanks to all their knowledge of the local market.

CHAPTER 8: HOW TO SCALE THE INVESTMENT

For most investors, the plan is to create a measurable, passive income engine. But you have to realize that you can't do it all by yourself. It's hard to give up control, but outsourcing a successful business is essential. Deciding when to relinquish control of a business's specific responsibility is an emotional decision. However, you can't do anything all by yourself. Often, scaling is a step up.

Portfolio scaling:

Buying your first property allows you to take all the emotional and financial resources you need. Evaluating every real estate and financial option, collecting your payments, sitting down and signing on dotted lines can feel like a great accomplishment. The property you just bought is the biggest investment you have ever made, and if it turns out good, you will be very proud of it. However, if you want to be a real estate investor, that first real estate deal is not the last. That is just the beginning. When the first investment begins to yield results, it is time to reinvest those gains or reinvest in the second, third, fourth and fifteenth asset. It is not easy, and will you be able to create a big real estate empire? Here are some great strategies that will help you expand your real estate realm as experts do:

Make a layout

Drive around town and look for "sale" signs in the front yard to find a great investment is not the best strategy. To find a great investment, you need to take an analytical view of the market. But before you do that, you need to be clear about what you want. What is the cost range of an investment property? Which annual return are you aiming for? What market are you interested in? What is your five-year plan? Your ten-year plan? Interested investors have a clear vision of what they want and have a clear plan to get there.

Build a better team

Expanding your real estate portfolio is not something you can do alone. Let's say you have a solid vision of the property you want to acquire. The first person you want to add to the team is a real estate agent. Experienced agents know every detail of the market, understand where the trends are going, anticipate fluctuations and are well connected to the local population. Without a good agent, there is no real estate portfolio. In the meantime, partnering with investment-focused real estate agents can quickly turn projects into profitable field operations. With an agent's insider knowledge of the market, your portfolio may grow faster than you think. And that was just the beginning. You need a good real estate lawyer to handle all your documents. If you are enriching your investment property, building a relationship with a trusted contractor can be beneficial.

You also need a good property manager to handle the rental charge. Like all big businesses, building a real estate empire should be a team effort.

Finance:

You have finished your research, and you now know what characteristics you want. You have worked hard and found the best people to build relationships with. What is left now is the most important part: money. If you are one of the lucky few, your agent will have enough money to start writing down all the great property checks you have. But most investors need funding. There are many finance options accessible to capitalists. Some of them are very regular, other very creative:

Traditional debt

The most common are regular loans. This is the bank mortgage we all know. 20% fall, fixed interest rate, 30-year period. The sub-portion of a traditional loan is usually 20% less pay. For most investors, this is outrageous. Fortunately, there are options that require little or no money.

Hard money

Hard money is private money, which explores the potential value of an investment, not the qualifications of the borrower. If the property you want to buy is a good bet in a hot market, you may find it difficult to finance the purchase.

However, as you can imagine, hard money comes with very difficult conditions. Everything is negotiable because it is a personal loan, and many hard-to-pay programs must be repaid within a year. Interest rates also vary from market rates to two or three times.

Crowdfunding

This is a new and innovative option that can deliver great results for smart marketing campaigns. Crowdfunding works by distributing large numbers of investors, often at very low levels, and estimating profits. This method can bring in a lot of money if you are to take advantage of it. Think of it as the intersection between REIT and Twitter. Expanding a real estate portfolio into a real estate realm is a big but achievable dream. Partnering with an experienced and knowledgeable real estate agent will make your dream come true quicker and easier. If you are serious about creating a real estate empire, contact us today!

CHAPTER 9: IMPACT OF COVID -19 ON REAL ESTATE

A Global Pandemic

Physical and social distancing have profoundly changed people's way of living and communicating, and the effects of this pandemic have brought down the demand for other forms of space, probably for the first time in recent history. This created a situation without precedent for the real estate industry. The longer this crisis lasts, the more likely we are to see positive and sustainable change in behavior, beyond the immediate state of emergency. In order to respond to Covid-19 's current challenge, and to help pave the way for coping with what could be structural adjustments after the crisis for the industry, real estate leaders must take action now.

Most would centralize cash management to concentrate on performance and to adjust the way they make decisions about portfolio and capital spending and most real estate operators were wise to start with decisions that guarantee the safety and health of all space owners, employees, tenants as well as others. The smartest will now also think about how to permanently change the real estate landscape in the long term, and will adjust their strategies.

However, safety providers struggle to minimize safety risks for both employees and consumers. In the meantime, many asset owners and operators are facing severely reduced gross profit and nearly all fear how many tenants will find it difficult to make their lease payments.

During the crisis not all real estate assets perform the same way. Assets with a higher human density appear to have had the hardest hit: hospitals, regional shopping centers, lodging, and apartment buildings have sold off significantly. Contrarily, facilities for self-storage, industrial facilities, and data centers experienced less substantial declines.

Public-health authorities could gradually change building codes to minimize the risk of future pandemics, possibly affecting HVAC requirements, square footage per person, and enclosed room amounts. Simultaneously, just as the baby boom generation age into the ideal range for independent and assisted living, fear of viral infections such as Covid-19 may encourage them to stay a bit longer in their current homes. Demand for senior living services could dampen, or the company might totally adjust to satisfy consumer demands for more physical space and more complex operating requirements. Early data from China suggests that they started to shift to e-commerce because of coronavirus, taking advantage of the situation.

Consumers forced to shop online due to closed shopping centers and malls can permanently change their purchasing habits toward e-commerce for some categories. Before the coronavirus outbreak, a lot of consumers were already starting to get away from physical stores. This long-term trend is likely to escalate much faster after the crisis, especially when many previously existing companies are tipped to failure or pressured to dramatically reduce their presence. Fairly limited asset classes may see an improvement in their economy, thanks to the demand that rises as more people work from home, while other asset classes can struggle.

What about real estate?

The COVID-19 outbreak and the consequential pandemic have intensified the need for structural changes, and have demonstrated that those who have not made those investments will definitely need to adapt quickly. Few real estate companies were developing digital and technological analytics strategies before Covid-19, but now such strategies are essential. Many immediate consequences of the epidemic include the need for constructive communication on health and safety in public environments for customers and workers. Following the coronavirus pandemic, real estate industry leaders have taken on a set of common considerations.

Owners and operators, above everything else, must protect people's lives and health by any fair means, ensuring everyone's safety. Leading operators must make sure to both completely recognize the interests of tenants at this moment and to secure everyone in their ecosystem. These improvements are the smartest thing to do, as they're also good for business: tenants and space users will remember your initiative, building a great and trustful relationship.

Creativity should also be used more often, since not all cash-creating practices need to involve cost cutting. For instance, some residential developers are looking for creative ways to liquidate new inventories, such as lease-to-own programs and funding collaborations.

Although it may be tempting to make reductive conclusions regarding the economic effects of the coronavirus pandemic, the corresponding policy responses across portfolios at the city, state and federal levels may not be universal. In order to produce insights about the local epidemiological and economic conditions, what is happening and the effect of the crisis on individual tenants, real estate leaders are taking advantage of the abundance of available behavioral data. Few real estate companies have knowledge on these topics, and far fewer have the right tools, procedures and accountabilities in order to make decisions.

The value of digitization has been magnified by physical, social distancing and lockdown itself, in particular thanks to interventions including tenant and client experience. Such innovative services could generate satisfaction and the opportunity to build entirely new business sources while serving the demands of tenants and end-users.

Many investors and operators are reconsidering all capital investments within the context of a post-coronavirus environment. Some have now turned their mindsets towards seeking single assets at discount prices, but the ongoing challenge in accessing capital markets has slowed the activity and the availability will remain limited as prospective buyers wait for valuations to recover.

Some landlords are now starting to think about what to do when the pandemic-induced crisis will be completely over. Instead of focusing on conventional economic or customer-survey-driven methods, real estate executives are searching for answers from economists, sociologists, futurists and technologists. They are wondering if employees will demand larger and safer workspaces, if people will fear living in condominiums if they will have to use elevators, etc. Of course, nowadays, everything is uncertain. But business leaders can begin to discover new and more reliable insights by employing an innovative staff and using new technological and digital methods, in order to be ready when everything will be finally over.

CONCLUS ION

For many, real estate is simple and simple to understand, and investment is easy because it involves a fair exchange between real estate owners (landlords) and real estate users (tenants). As long as the hot water continues to flow and the rent arrives at the right time, everyone is happy. However, real estate investing is more complex because a variety of real estate investments, such as commercial, industrial, residential, are traded on stock exchanges known as REITs. The goal when investing in real estate is to invest in today's jobs and grow and make more money in the future. You need to get enough profit or "return" to cover the risks you take, the taxes you pay and the costs of owning a real estate investment, such as utilities and insurance.

If you are considering buying a property, whether it is your family's primary residence or an investment property, you need to know how to make your payment secure and easy to access. As a new investor, have you ever wondered what equity or real estate are best? Both have some strengths and weaknesses, but the answer depends on your personality and preferences, just like your portfolio and circumstances. One of the most common ways to own real estate is through a special type of investment called REIT

(Real Estate Investment Trust). Real estate investment trusts have an almost endless "flavor." For example, some invest only in commercial real estate, while others only invest in apartment buildings. REITs can be traded in the same way as securities through securities company accounts, and dividends are taxed differently than dividends of shares. Find out how REITs work and whether you should consider owning a REIT instead of real estate.

Some credit counsellors will send additional payments to your creditors to reduce your real estate debt. Instead, you will be asked to have more money on hand so that you can save a good amount of emergency funds. You rarely have a real estate investment directly in your name! In most cases, serious real estate investors own real estate known as a Limited Liability Company or LLC. This special type of company can protect personal property from litigation and other risks. In fact, most wealthy investors own homes through a risk management practice. As a new real estate investor, it is imperative to understand how the LLC works and why it is used to keep rental properties and other real estate investments.

One of the biggest investments one can make in life is their primary residence. Unfortunately, considering the costs of insurance, maintenance, net mortgage interest, and other expenses, some new investors/homeowners do not realize that the real return rate after home inflation is about 0%. You need to open your eyes and make your first major real estate investment.

START UP &
BUSINESS MANAGEMENT

Entrepreneurship and small business guide:
how to manage your social media, marketing,
ethics public policy and finally sell your brand.

Special focus on food & beverage

catering is one of the most powerful and widespread and explanatory examples of commercial activities carried out medium-small commercial properties

CHAPTER 1: BUSINESS FOOD & BEVERAGE AND ENTERTAINMENT

WHAT IS A COMMERCIAL ACTIVITY

We have talked during our theme of the commercial real estate part especially from the point of view of the investment on the property, but there is a part, not secondary attached to this branch, which deals more specifically with what can be done within these properties, ie commercial activities. Commercial activities are practically "the tenant who pays the rent of commercial properties", that is, the companies that manage the content within a property.

In this typology, among the best known activities we certainly find bars, restaurants, hotels and entertainment venues. They are among the "medium-small size" activities: for example, in larger areas we can find supermarkets / hypermarkets or, in smaller sizes, we can think of a professional studio or the typical retail store. Speaking of size, I am referring right now to the average extension in meters that an activity of those sectors can contemplate:

instead the "size" at company level or the generation of monetary flows is different: in that case the extension is not always indicative because other types of factors intervene, which explain to us if an activity can be more or less profitable and therefore define its size in economic terms.
The most common investor, and in any case a good part of the market for those who do business in commercial activities, often directs their attention towards the restaurant, or "food & beverage" and entertainment sector, which is the most commercial. and widespread: probably the most important of all exercises. In our analysis, approximating by default, we will focus more on this type of sector, even if the general rules that we will then outline often apply a little to all businesses without distinction.

WHO IS THE SUBJECT THAT ASSEMBLES A COMMERCIAL ACTIVITY

Normally there are two subjects when we deal with commercial properties: first of allthe owner of the property, which depending on the importance of the investment can be a small owner of some store, rather than a magnate with considerable potential or professional companies that they deal with construction or commercial investments. The second subject that appears, which is a bit the protagonist of this part of the book, is the tenant who can be, likewise, a small trader, rather than an affluent restaurateur with various points of sale (think of franchises) up to the big companies or tycoons that manage large hotel chains and supermarkets, for example. We have talked about two subjects, summarizing, owner of the property and **tenant**, because especially in small businesses the two locations are almost always distinct. Many times, however, they coincide, either because the manager of the business has "grown so much" that he was able to buy the property where he carries out the same (or in many cases various properties to replicate and scale his business model), or, looking at him from another point of view, because 'large companies have thought (in addition to building) to delegate: a part of their capital and human resources in this case will be dedicated exclusively to the direct management and administration of their companies, in the same properties they own. In these cases, obviously, we are not already talking about two subjects, but the subject is practically the same and economically and financially it has a logical sense of easy intuition: on the one hand, reducing costs, because if we look at it for the business side, it is it is completely different to go from paying a rent (disposable), to paying the installment of a mortgage, for example, to buy your own property. So seen from the side of the business, the step of buying a property to carry it out is almost always positive, when the position is openly favorable, because it "lightens the balance sheet" spread over several years with depreciation and a complete sense, ie squaring the circle, to corporate life. Seen instead from the point of view of the magnate who, for example, builds a large hotel (and then instead of entrusting it to a tenant in management, he decides to create his own directory to administer it personally), it is a choice that outlines the intention not to base your investment on a passive perspective (collecting the rent without doing any other action), but to take the path of a further investment on the investment and take the risk of setting up one's own business: if it is profitable, you will evidently benefit from the volume of business generated . In the latter case, it is clearly necessary to have a considerable economic strength to take on a double risk or such a demanding economic commitment; you also need very well-rooted skills within the business that you are going to organize, because the success of all the global investment depends on the outcome. In fact, should the activity not be profitable, not only would there be a loss of earnings (for passive rents), but there would be many other problems in the balance sheet: in that case the only way out would be to fall back on the management of a third party who carries out the same activity in a profitable way, and that allows the tycoon to return to have positive revenues, through the mere rent of the property. In the best case, there is also the hypothesis that << the big fish meets an even bigger one >> who wants to buy both the business and the property. If, on the other hand, neither of the two exit-strategy hypotheses described above occurs, our tycoon would begin to have significant economic problems.

WHAT COMES TO INSTALL A COMMERCIAL ACTIVITY

As an entrepreneur, I can safely tell you that setting up a business is one of the most risky things of all, among all the entrepreneurial categories, because it involves significant disbursements, implies advanced knowledge, requires the assistance of professionals and employees. Furthermore, it is necessary to guess, the place, the moment and the right system to dominate the competition, and many other things; and to make matters worse, an entrepreneur can do everything perfectly, but the possibility of "strange astral conjunctures" remains, so things don't work the same and crash, or they work but they don't give the desired results and therefore are insufficient to amortize the 'investment. Yes, because it is an investment: investing time, money and resources in a company: if all goes well, costs are amortized, wages and fees are paid and a dividend remains at the end of the year; the purpose of all this is practically to pay the expenses and have minimal earnings, increasing during the value of that brand or organization (to then resell it and have further earnings).

But what if things go wrong? If in 2020 for example we are forced to close our company 3 months for thecovid-19? Will the once profitable business continue to be profitable or will it survive? The virus was a bad thing for the economy, but the economy thrives on ups and downs, real estate crises, financial crises, crises of any kind. They are called risks and an investor must keep in mind that they exist: nobody could imagine a world pandemic that would actually slow down or block the economy of hundreds of countries in the world. Pero 'has arrived, as well as past and future wars, and many other disasters, but economic activities have always continued to exist, because there are very entrepreneurial people who calculate everything, even that things can go wrong, and therefore they know that << today you win and tomorrow you lose >>, as in a long footballchampionship, where maybe a team starts less favored, but then comes back and wins. And if he doesn't win there will be another adventure to undertake, another championship.

So the question is to do things measured, planned and well, and above all not to do them at random, like most people who, when they are tired of doing a certain job, suddenly one day they wake up and with all naivety, they convince themselves that they are the great cheffsfor example, or the largest investors on the planet in any commercial field: they invest all their savings in randomly botched activities and often find themselves short of liquidity', because "an entrepreneur does not is invented "from today to tomorrow: they are just reckless attempts, and without any logic and destined for a crash, for an expert eye who recognizes them in advance only by how they are set.

WHAT YOU NEED TO KNOW TO SET UP A BUSINESS

I continue to insist that the first necessary requirement is to know what it is aboutn the course of my professional activity I am seeing too many small or self-employed companies operating in random circumstancesor with a really very deficient organization. This way of doing as well as being a losing well in terms of savings, proves to be a boomerang that will affect their lives, self-esteem and of course their savings, because the business has excellent chances of "falling apart". Absolutely, the first requirement is therefore to **be an expert in the business** that you are going to assemble, and certainly an enthusiast and lover of that world, up to know its more detailed facets. The second indispensable requirement is to **have the savings or liquidity to undertake;** very important thing to mark as a basic rule << if a company requires an investment of 100, get hold of 150 or 200 >>, because 'reserves could be needed in negative periods, in market fluctuations, in unexpected events, using them to keep it floating. Otherwise there is the possibility of arriving to lose everything. It is madness to buy an asset that has a cost equal to the available capital: it would mean that you are moving beyond your means.

Below we list all the other necessary requirements:

- **Check the current regulations:** cit. << with the help of a professional, contact the municipality of residence to request the permits necessary for the activity to be carried out. Through technical consultancy define criteria and rules and what can be done (and what can't), at the structural and plant engineering level. It is absolutely essential, in order not to risk making irreparable mistakes, to work authorized and in peace 'and to have clear ideas also in terms of costs and project>>.
- **Licenses:** acquire the main and accessory licenses necessary to carry out a regular activity. When

working without a license or border-line, it could be profitable in the short run, but apart from committing an infringement, it absolutely will not be profitable in the long run let alone in the resale phase. There is a distinction to be made on licenses: if we return to catering for a moment as an example, there are obvious differences between having a bar, restaurant or disco license for example, or a hotel. For each area there are general and even municipal indications, on the basis the entrepreneur will have to comply with the requirements, so that the license is granted. And then, more on the technical side, there are category or safety limitations that determine the "goodness" of a deal. Not only that, according to the type, the days and times of opening change, but also the possibility of offering one service rather than another and also in detail the conformation of the commercial activity, which must be adapted to the rules according to the influx of people, location, and type of service to be performed. We will deepen this theme when we technically talk about how to prepare or renovate a commercial space.

- **Know how:** as the word says it is "the art of knowing how to do it": it is something that, either you know why you are experts in that profession (and have acquired the right skills), or that you must buy and it has costs. Together with the license and the trade fund, it is one of the main discriminants that determine the value of an activity. The easiest example to understand is the recipe for the best pizza or the best ice cream. Everyone makes pizzas and ice cream. But, have you ever wondered <<why the whole city goes to pour in those usual two places, and nobody ever goes to the other 50? >> The answer is << because 'they have the best recipe for that product, and anyway the one that most like the market>>. So that "know-how" has a value and they can keep it secret (and continue to dominate the competition) or they can sell it by teaching third parties to do the same thing.

- **Commercial fund:** we mentioned it so we explain it in detail. In reality it is not necessary to start a new business; but it is essential to create it during the life of the company. We are speaking in a nutshell of the volume of business, or more simply of the "real customers who have a business": translated into numbers, of the volume of liquid revenue that these customers produce. The trade fund can be real (represented by the balance sheet and the volume of business expressed in a calendar year), or it can be potential, that is, the company's ability to expand and improve. Needless to say, the real trade fund is paid (and even salty at times) when the purchase of a business is perfected, while the potential is << like a great pair of shoes that are worn only for a wedding >>: you know it's there, you know it's worth it, but you'll never know if you can use it. In fact, the most important thing in the event of a transfer of ownership, with a significant outlay of capital, is to defend and confirm the numbers of the previous years: it is reasonable to think that new customers can be acquired, but old ones can be equally hypothesized that they can also be lost if you do not operate properly.

Once these priority aspects have been studied, what you need to set up a company depends on the activity you want to undertake: some will require **machinery** and **technical equipment,** others will also need **furnishings** and every aspect that has to do with the facade "on the public". Obviously, during the evaluation of an activity they are an important point and with a peculiarity: they almost never devalue (at least strictly speaking of machinery and technical equipment) and the reason is that they can be dismantled or moved and used in another store. , and therefore also be sold separately to similar companies.

Aspects to be kept in mind will then be the strategy of investing time and resources to increase the value of a **brand or commercial name:** if the business is newly established it will have to build an image and a reputation in its sector of competence: if instead it deals with a sale of activities,the brand becomes part of the negotiation, with the evident attribution of a certain value to be quantified.

Let's not forget that, to start a business, if we are not owners of the property, we will have to find a rental agreement with the seller. It will be done on a multi-year basis to give the entrepreneur the opportunity to amortize the costs, and if he has a solid company, the benefit will be mutual, because the owner will thus guarantee an annuity, which can even be spent during the financing phase. of another building initiative, and obviously the investor will have time to repay his capital and generate a profit.

WHAT MAKES AN ACTIVITY WINNING

<< Position, position, position >>: you have to repeat it until you get tired, especially because for wrong price logics, many times you try to save money at the expense of the fundamental thing, undermining the investment from the ground up.

An important place then occupies the image, namely the brand and the attractiveness of the store from a strategic and aesthetic point of view (we will deal extensively in the second appendix with this theme).

Here we summarize the three fundamental pillars of an enterprise:

- **Product:** there is no profitable activity without a strong product that can outperform the competition, be it a physical product (such as making ice cream) or emotional (such as making fun). The product must always have the best value for money and follows the laws on supply and demand according to the location where it is undertaken. The banality of a product, the scarcity in quality terms or the price out of the logic of the market can alone sink any company, therefore in the planning phase they are very important strategies to be outlined in a long-term plan.
- **Service:** we can offer the best product in the world, and also have little competition, but if there is a lack of service, it could affect sales. To optimize and best express the potential of a company, you must have strong organizational skills and put all the cardsin their place. You need to know how to bargain the staff, in number and in quality, better to replicate the

product in a scalar and systematic form. So not only must you be able to express a one-timeproduction, but to repeat it, using people and means in order to generate lasting numbers over time, through effective and satisfactory quality standards, which are able to further enhance the product itself .

- **Planning:** it is possible to have the best product and the best service, but if you "sleep on your laurels", other people can overcome this model and become important and serious competitors to the point of even surpassing those who had wonderful ideas. The durability of the company over time is one of the most important things ever: short-term policies must be implemented, aimed at acquiring liquidity, but above all we must think "in the long run": when there are important outlays of money, in fact, there is a long-term amortization to always keep in mind and, before starting to make net gains, you must be able to last as long as possible, primarilyto cover the investment costs. This can be gradual with gains over time, up to the achievement of the goal or can be resolved with a re-sale of the activity that covers all expenses and produces a profit.

In planning I also want to mention two very important subtitles such as **strategic choices and competition analysis.** Both are long-term policies and must be applied during the investment planning phase, before taking the field The strategic choices are all those decisions which, based on experience and skills, must be made to study and classify the most important issues concerning planning: location for example. To be clearer, first when we talked about << position, position, position >> we were referring to first-rate, top-quality geo-localizations: to always be in front, in a geographical sense, but also of marketing positioning. Here instead, more specifically speaking of location I want to refer to this specific example: << our store is geographically correctly positioned in the city center; it even has an important and successful brand and in social networks there is a lot of talk about us. Why don't we have the desired results? >>.

Provided that product, service, and all quality-price standards are correct, there may be reasons related to the point of sale or to the competition that have not been correctly evaluated:

- LOCATION: there is no unique guarantee of success, setting up a shop in the so-called "center". Always betrayed by the logic of price, aimed at saving money, many times I have seen choosing stores, not exactly in the center: I would say that << there is a center and a center!>>. Speaking to the inexperienced entrepreneur, he often tells you that his shop is perfectly located, but once you have made a simple inspection, it is quite easy and disheartening to see how his are "false illusions". To determine a centric area, it is not enough to take a map and draw a circle with a defined radius. The roads are not all the same, and even the same road does not guarantee the same productivity at the bottom rather than at the head The assessments are always to be done in a physical and three-dimensional way, seeing the real situation. Even shops, which are side by side, we often notice that they have different profitability even if they do "the same job". The reason why one works (or not) can lead us back to the goodness of the management and the product-service, but many times the reason is purely linked to the property: a shop that makes a corner, rather than one with few windows, does not have not at all the same potential profitability. The same goes between a restaurant with a terrace, rather than exclusively indoors, or that has more or less seats: attention, then you have to convert this potential with other qualities. Often you have the skills but the location does not help due to the physical or organizational limits that it imposes on us. So a profound analysis during the design-purchase phase is by no means secondary, with experts who are able to anticipate, on the basis of their experience, certain situations which would then occur later, when it may already be late: when a shop is set up in a bad location it is difficult to remedy.

- COMPETITION: we never underestimate our competitors because one day they might not represent a factor, or another yes: let's not forget that they could sell the business to someone more proactive than they, or they could try to copy us, dispersing the customers and lowering our profits. In general, competition is something to always evaluate before undertaking, so as not to build a cathedral in the desertor on the contrary in the midst of other cathedrals all similar. One of the most innovative aspects that almost everyone underestimates, or does not contemplate, is the "exploitation of competition": it is a phenomenon that can be widely seen in large cities or large entertainment areas, and which deserves separate reflections. I am thinking of the typical example, in the reconversion in large metropolises of what were once "the ancient markets": today they are leisure centers with restaurants, shows and much more; these are real huge buildings, but they can also be streets or areas, where a series of bars and restaurants or discos accumulate: all, with the various differences, offer a little the same product, namely, fun. But let's take a more practical example: hypermarkets, which bring together a huge amount of retail stores, many of them similar in product and price line. This is a typical example of <<how to make a negative aspect like competition become a strength>>. The reason is very simple: a user is attracted by all the various possibilities offered by that situation and above all by comfort (is it another facet of the location: a place in a pedestrian area or a place with a private parking? A place easy to reach or an isolated place so as not to disturb the noises? All variables to be weighed in advance). So, most of the users go in search of those situations because << not even very clear what they are looking for >>, but they know they will find them: like when you go to a multi-screen cinema and decide the film at the moment to see: traditional cinema has disappeared.

So how do you work when you put yourself in such a market? Exactly as before, with the same rules and even more attention to quality and price to be competitive. We must certainly pay attention to the fact that the offer is not saturated for a certain type of product, with too many people undertaking in the same field or with similar products, and it is absolutely necessary to differentiate decisively by brand and service. Normally in this type of reality the models of francisingare distinguished because they are highly competitive models, designed to proceed in certain ways and with certain pricing policies. So what is the fault of a leisure center? Although it is true that a model of this type helps and relieves an investor from the burden of attracting people within 1 KM of him, then it is also true that if he does not differentiate himself and does not have something highly competitive, he is destined to succumb even more fiercely. Then there is another negative point: if the center, the road or the area is not well managed, not well geo-located or not well advertised, working in a model of this type is even more complicated, because attracting people to 1 KM from your shop, then it becomes a necessity and very often, the possible bad image of the area is confused with the image of the store, and therefore the latter will have serious billing problems, as it will be difficult to convey the clientele in an unfamiliar or unwelcome place.

BUSINESS RISK

We have mentioned the possibility in which things do not go in the right direction: each type of activity assumes a different business risk, which depends on a virtual calculation on the volume of capital employed, on the economic period, and on the type of product or service. It is clear that the same business risk cannot be attributed to a family restaurant that operates in a property owned, rather than a hotel, which perhaps asks third parties for a concession to manage a certain number of years. There are therefore **companies of high risk or of lower risk:** those of high risk are all those that follow trends, for example (in terms of definition, they come and go) and when clearly we are then working out of context, unless that you don't have the strength to do it, you can have significant problems. Other risky activities are those that have very strict regulations or a license that is not completely defined or that protects them from any disputes. The regulations unfortunately change over time and those who do not have everything expressly guaranteed and outlined could suffer problems related to bureaucracy or the changes that occur for economic or urban reasons. Even "news" or start-ups are high-risk activities: when you market a product that is innovative, it could work and become a fashion product (and therefore be very speculative), but it may also not work and therefore then and It is also difficult to correct the strategy in the race because the peculiarity that should have been a distinctive feature, then ends up also affecting a possible change. Without a doubt, however, there are as always in the life of the "workhorses" or evergreens that always work well or badly, that is, they have already been tried and tested over the years in different geographical areas and in different markets and are increasingly more or less profitable: residential real estate market, let's take an example to explain the concept, a long-term rental of an apartment compared to a "holiday rental": the first is undoubtedly a less bombastic and productive investment than the second, but with lower costs and with a practically minimal risk, in addition to being a safe haven asset, in comparison with the other type which is absolutely high risk.

COSTS, REVENUES, EARNINGS

This part is practically a small lesson on basic economics. We know that **costs** are all the expenses we use in carrying out a business: purchases, machinery, goods, personnel and everything else. Very often we forget to talk about the weather. **Time is one of the costs** most underrated in history. My innovative proposal is that << the time cost was included in the financial statements of companies >>: the result would be devastating, because many entrepreneurs would realize how little productive their organization is. The cost of time is practically "all the time lost and the capital invested" and blocked in an entrepreneurial activity: that is, the value that these would have if invested in another completely different initiative, or even in extreme cases in doing nothingIt is a modern version of the opportunity costand would allow us to understand "how many things had to be renounced" by spending time and resources in one company at the expense of another, but also of the family, or personal interests. Many times we focus so much on work that << for the anxiety of earning 100 we lose 150 >>; if we did the math well, perhaps it would turn out that there would have been enough, for a full life, a figure lower than that which we already had at the beginning, without facing any business risk. So when you are alone in front of the mirror, with a pen and a writing padlet's remember to put everything under the heading costs, because leaving out certain aspects, not secondary, usually make up the accounts and are always positive even when they are not.

Revenues are the income that our business produces, but they are "false friends": especially in the retail trade, they give the impresario the impression of being well, of having solid revenues and resources; we must however remember that these are not because they are a partial datum; we cannot spend everything we collect. Revenues are used to cover costs and to reinvest, and then only ultimately to make a profit. So there are absolutely no liquids available, but they are resources to be handled with absolute intelligence. A bad management of the revenues can absolutely sink the goodness of acommercial activityand to go to intervene then there are always only two ways: either to reinvest to increase the turnover, and therefore to try that the cost-revenues relationship is more favorable; or cut costs (which is sometimes healthy to avoid unnecessary shopping); but when you get "to the bone", you cannot always touch them, not to undermine the correct functioning of the company. Finally, **the earnings** are therefore the positive result of a work path made profitably: if there are no earnings, the road is uphill, unless you are in a phase of physiological recession or you just have initiated or re-invested.

These three economic factors are always to be looked at from a medium-long term perspective and for this there are the financial statements, which are nothing more than the summaries by period of exercise, of the actions taken by a company. You should never ever confuse revenues with earnings: if, for example, a bar collects 1000 euros a day, remember the operator who does not have 1000 euros to spend in his pocket, but only earned the residual after taking out expenses such as: staff, electricity and water, materials, taxes, that day's depreciation of machinery, depreciation of its initial investment, rents, time, and a lot of other costs. Sometimes making this calculation we find ourselves with the understanding that it’s not worth the risk.

Both corporate restructuring and reprogramming have well-defined rules and balances >> LV

CHAPTER 2: TOTAL RENOVATION OF A VS BAR - STAGING PROPERTY, WITH THE ABILITY TO REPROGRAM

DIFFERENCE BETWEEN RESTRUCTURING AND REMODELING

The investor of a business is normally a person with experience in the sector, and when this is not the case, normally he joins a company with someone who brings this essential value. Unfortunately, however, there are more and more people who re-invent themselves without any experience and, even worse, with resources below the minimum required level, they venture into companies that they then cannot carry out; most of the time due to lack of funds, or to changes in the market or lack of experience and planning. Always making the right example of catering, one of the most common and widespread mistakes is that, in addition to re-inventing oneself as restaurateurs, to believe oneself as great architects or interior designers, and even marketing experts, with results often not up to par and heavy consequences also from an economic point of view, the error or the principle is always the same: the savings policy. We have already mentioned that in commercial real estate "who spends more spends better", if we look at it from the perspective of the investment: because by buying something of value, we present ourselves to our personal race with the competition equipped with a Ferrari and not with a small car to compete. If the logic of savings can be endorsed (but absolutely not married because there are very specific logics and rules also in that field) with a residential property, for its flexibility and for the fact of having a more standard, common and numerous user , on the other hand, with a commercial property (whether during the purchase of the property itself or during the planning of an activity), one must not remain "too short", in order not to make choices of secondary locations, accept obvious structural defects, or any factor that could potentially penalize our initiative; in this case the losses would be incalculable and the fate inexorably marked. Therefore, the selection of the property is important, among many in the different areas, taking into account all the factors that we discussed earlier in relation to the potentially profitable business. If in doubt about a position at the expense of another, it is always advisable to contact a professional in the sector to see the different possibilities or choices that the market offers, and to weigh the goodness of one area at the expense of another.

Once the content has been chosen, we then move on to a second phase which is decisive and then let's talk about what to put in the chosen shop: depending on the situations we will have to evaluate whether the store needs a radical change, which also affects installations and structure, or if it needs only a superficial reprogramming, intervening only superficially in the aspect visible to the public. In catering this type of intervention I like to call it **bar-staging,** which would be the commercial version of home-staging of houses, although with a considerable difference: what I mean as bar-staging is not limited only to the aesthetic aspect, perhaps accompanied by a programmatic evaluation of the type of investment and annuity to be assembled. In this case we are talking about something much more profound because the choice of colors or arrangement of a room or marketing or arrangement of furniture and resources can directly influence the increase in that company's revenues. We think of a beginner who decorates the bar, who has just bought, with very flat colors, tone on tone or even worse with colors that do not marry at all, and (without considering at the moment the range of the countless other choices he has to make on disposition, materials, machinery, lights, decorations...) he finds himself with a dull, monotonous and cheesy appearance bar, which certainly does not provide the right welcome and gives the impression of little professionalism. Let's think about how many times the same bar was subsequently sold to a brilliant and experienced entrepreneur who changed little and nothing (or on the contrary changed everything), and converted it into a gold mine:evidently this was a coincidence where the location was not so bad, but the subsequent choices made by the first investor were wrong. We can therefore say that those who have real experience, and real competence, can sometimes try to make up for it only and also dedicate themselves to an activity that is not completely his; in most cases one should rely on a professional in the sector to avoid making certain typical mistakes and above all to characterize and set up the store well.

For example, all supermarkets have real teamsof people who dedicate themselves specifically to that: they do nothing but study, optimize and propose new spaces, new colors, new situations; they even often change the shelves because "behind" there is an economic reasoning and they have perhaps studied that certain products are sold more if placed at the bottom rather than at the top If people who work at certain levels pay "good money" for what might seem like nonsense to most, because the novice investor who is starting now with commercial real estate or a business, decides heinously takes an additional risk and without experience, organize and decorate your own point of sale at random, or according to your personal logic? This would be very good if he bought a private house and wanted to live there: that he organizes it as he wishes, but then, if he were wrong, to pay duty during the sale, because people of common sense might not like it. But in the "commercial" it is not possible to reason according to a perspective of tastes, but of sales

<< So we can define the necessary or vital restructuring or bar-stagingin a commercial property, to characterize its activity and to optimize revenues >>.

But when to use one rather than the other technique? This varies greatly depending on the activity rather than the location and the need to prepare the store according to the law and according to the necessary safety standards. In general it can be said that: when there is a change of license or a change of activity, for reasons of law, but also for reasons of opportunity and updating of the property, an integral restructuring is carried out, perhaps negotiating with the owner of the property that still has to give consent. The concept of bar-stagingin spite of the name, applicable to all types of commercial activity, can be applied in all cases where you continue with the same type of license and no technical changes are required by legislation, and you simply want to give a shot of image and important substance to a store, to show first that things have changed, and later, to be able to express an economic revaluation of the store and the present activity, with consequent improvements from the point of view view of the entrances. We reiterate the importance of avoiding the do-it-yourselfwhich normally gives birth to anonymous stores, based on the logic of savings, which are not very functional at the time of working and replicating the product in a form that produces profitability.

If in the purchase of a house it was essential to evaluate the state of conservation of the property, in commercial properties it begins to be secondary because it is almost taken for granted that they will then be distorted or arranged and therefore we tend to market rustic properties, or finished but completely diaphanous and with standardized installations which can then be adapted to most commercial companies.

STEPS FOR AN INTEGRAL RESTRUCTURING

We have already seen how the first step is absolutely an analysis of the state of the property, not according to aesthetic criteria, but according to the expected updates necessary in a long period for installations according to the law.

Here are the most significant steps of an integral restructuring, the order of which is by no means secondary, because many times, those who are not experts in this sector, start for the half or for the end, and then find themselves redoing all in another way; needless to say, in doing so there is a huge increase in time and costs and often jeopardizing the previous work or the final result.

- **Check the current regulations:** << with the help of a professional, contact the municipality of residence to request the necessary permits for the intervention. Through technical advice, define criteria and rules and what can be done (and what not), at the structural and plant engineering level. It is absolutely fundamental, in order not to risk making irreparable mistakes, to work authorized and in peace 'and to have clear ideas also in terms of costs and project. Recommended inspection for all technicians who will have to work: architect, master worker, electrician and plumber >>.

- **Study the new distribution of the spaces:** << compatibly with the project first of all define where the technical spaces of the bathroom and kitchen are located, and then concentrate on the main areas such as lounge or terraces or leisure space. You need to be very clear where to locate sensitive spaces before starting work, because all installations depend on it and, cascading, realizing belatedly an error can be impossible to solve or very expensive >>.

Particular attention, however, to the local policy: never underestimate the entry and the hypothetical distribution of the production points. The entrance is the business card of a store and must be large, attractive and easily accessible. Stores that have a bad entrance or architectural barriers are certainly having trouble billing large numbers. He must also be intelligent, and move the customer towards the most attractive and important we have. Sensitive production spaces are the most important spaces after technical spaces: the first inevitably affect the distribution of the store, but these are the ones that will discriminate whether we sell or not. In the very intuitive example of a bar, it is vitally important where the counter (and kitchen) is placed for example: not only that, the collections can change according to the size of the counter, the shape, the color, the comfort and the type of session (or not) that you set; follows a lot the logics about the types of bars that are going to be built, therefore an expert will not only look at aesthetic criteria, but also of consistency and functionality at work in order to increase the takings.

- **Demolition:** << is the first active phase of the work. We will have already studied whether there are old walls to be demolished or old installations to be abandoned. At this stage it is appropriate to protect or remove the furniture and parts that you intend to save, so as not to damage them because it normally produces really annoying dusts at the time of cleaning and inconveniences due to the work of several people in the same environment. It is appropriate to clear the area as much as possible to facilitate the work and then be able to easily intervene in the removal of doors and fixtures or demolition of walls, decommissioning of furniture that is of no interest and anything else. If the wooden floor, for example, is one of the things that can be saved, protect it to avoid direct scarring for moving furniture or even unwanted, for the simple passage with the possibility of small debris under the shoes >>. Of course it is true that unlike what happens in residential property, as we have highlighted, there is a tendency to have diaphanous spaces in order to avoid demolitions but go directly to a redistribution of spaces with internal divisions.

- **Construction of new walls:** << if provided, there will be the redistribution of the surface with new walls that will delimit the new size of the rooms. According to the uses, they can be made with blocks, with wood or with the most economic and widespread solution and with the best aesthetic result: the plasterboard, properly insulated >>.

Also in this case, the choice of distribution and separations in a commercial property is far from trivial: it must respect certain logics of breadth and design, above all to give users a feeling of being able to breathe. Therefore preference for diaphanous spaces, even if we record that in certain activities, the separation of some more intimate environments can be a stylistic choice, but also an economic one, sometimes important: we think of a reserved and intimate room in a restaurant or certain delicious corners, for to offer customers certain differences in atmosphere, or if we think of the economic side we think of discos and prive': we offer exclusive services, with an increase in management costs for the company, in exchange for notoriously higher prices for the service offered in that space: these are details that aim to differentiate customers and to have a different economic entrance.

- **Electrician and plumber:** < < contact the electrician and plumber who, assisted by a worker, will have to "cut" the walls and the floor and then channel their pipes. Both technicians will have to prepare the installations according to the law and according to the project, using the appropriate materials, and trace their installations from the command point to the central plant. The electrician will have to discuss about how you want to equip and equip the house to understand the necessary power and adapt an authorized electrical panel, then making the related requests to the administration company. Both will propose ideal points of water and light in the most common points, according to their criterion, but here also the user will have to give his opinion according to his needs and the result will be a mix of requests, standards and advice on the basis of experience of other previous works. Also contact specialized technicians, for example that of air conditioners to have the desired machinery ready > >.

The main difference between residential and commercial property is that commercial property systems are often "exposed", both for a significant reduction in the cost of the work, and because they are lost to sight in the large space or can be camouflaged in full industrial-style aesthetic, quite cleared through customs today.

- **Carpenter, installer, tiler, gas engineer, carpenter:**<< call these skilled workers for the realization of works that cannot be damaged, even if you continue to work in the house. Barriers, stairs, ornaments, counter-ceilings, bathroom and kitchen tiles, floors can be made only if it is not a delicate surface that can be damaged, such as for example wood and similar surfaces: in this case it is expected that almost everyone has finished and poses, or alternatively poses and covers themselves to protect it, but at the risk of ruining it. Similarly, the first finishes and details can be made. There is always to keep in mind that if you choose a so-called floating floor, that is superimposed on the existing floor, this installation must be done before commissioning the doors because the height of the floor will obviously vary and consequently also the size of the new doors to be requested on assignment. Normally we tend to leave the change of doors and windows last (being able for safety reasons), so as not to run the risk of ruining new materials due to the great coming and going of people and above all the transport and assembly of new furniture or antique furniture that had been moved. The fixtures and doors and walls are then finished with the relative skirting boards or decorations, which have the function of protecting the materials and hiding any cutting or installation defects >>.

- **Painter:** << normally he is the last to arrive and is in charge of fixing all the small defects and then covering them first with white, and then giving personality to the house with color. In theory, he should paint in white before the assembly of the new furniture and once mounted, dedicate himself to color: this would facilitate the times and the task of the painter, but if it were not possible, you can do everything later >>.

Unlike what happens for residential properties, here the painter must be much more an artist than a performer always maintaining certain quality standards, he must collaborate with the investor and the designer to find suitable chromatic solutions that reflect the distinctive features of the company, and therefore have to do with a defined marketing strategy, and then highlight the important points depending on the activity to be carried out. Therefore it must make more quantities and be effective; maybe he can afford to be slightly less shrewd (as opposed to what happens in the residential field), because what will be decisive is the general appearance of the intervention.

- **Furniture, lights, decorations:** last but not least, we find the fun, but not secondary, part of beautifying the place: many people often do it "by chance" by mixing styles, colors and materials that are inconsistent and ruining something that it was thought and that it had an important cost.

If it is important in homes, a detailed study is essential in the premises:

- LIGHTS: they must take into account also and above all consumption (as well as all the machinery with which we supply the premises) because there are companies that count many opening hours; luckily the technology comes together offering a great variety of neon or led lights, with great energy savings and aesthetic solutions and colors of all kinds. In general, then there is to reflect on warm or cold lights depending on the type of work that will be carried out. Needless to say, cold lights are generally brighter and also highlight the flaws in the room; warm lights are generally used more for night activities because they also affect the atmosphere of the store.

- FURNITURE: the furnishing of a shop consists of everything that is visible to the public, and therefore contemplates any seating, leisure space, entrance, public service spaces such as exhibitors or counters and customer attention. All these visible spaces must be arranged in a functional way, in order to allow the correct performance of the activity and respect a certain aesthetic taste.

There is no doubt that there are situations in which machinery, in certain industry styles, is sometimes integrated into the concept of commercial real estate as part of the furniture: we think of the large vacuums located in large supermarkets or shops, so powerful and invasive to the eye that over time have made fashion, marking a style of commercial property with exposed systems. We think of a brewery or a large professional wine cellar, where sometimes there are even real cisterns at sight and guided tours are organized to explain the various stages of processing. Even in a restaurant, for example, there is a pizzeria area or an "open" kitchen area, and therefore in these cases there is the transformation of the technical space into an absolute first floor space inside a room. It is obvious that for these reasons it must be located and designed so as to be easy and at the same time to have an aesthetic function.

_ DECORATIONS: decorations are all those accessory elements that give personality and uniqueness to a shop. They may be some particular furniture or lights with the function of drawing attention, but also paintings, statues, vases, areas, original details aimed at creating a kind of context or choreography. They must be harmonious with the rest and characterize the store so that it is attractive and original for customers. The keywords in this area are balance and consistency: decorating with something that loads the environment too much is harmful. Everything must have a harmonious shape and be noticed with the right importance. If something is not noticed, neither individually nor does it serve to contextualize a specific choreography, this often means that it is too much.

- **Exterior of the room:** << it is the only item that can be independent from the rest and can have a non-consequential value: that is, it can be reformed or not even later or in a different time space. According to the technical characteristics of the house, it is necessary to intervene on roofs, façades, gardens, entrances, accessory spaces and gates. Clearly this type of intervention requires "a whole separate discussion" which is not part of the themes of this book, but has much more to do with architecture >>.

The exterior of a commercial premises must also have the function of drawing attention. It must include **a sign** with the distinctive features of the company, whose characteristics must be aesthetic and also highly visible. The name and logos of the business will be on the sign and the type of product or service it offers must be clear.

We have already talked about the importance of the **entrance,** which characterizes the transition between exterior and interior.

We have already mentioned the fact that it is advisable to have accessory spaces outside the store, which will be exploited according to the activity; but one of the almost essential things of a commercial property is the ease of **parking.** In fact, if it is true that there are properties of this type also in pedestrian areas (where however there are always paid parking lots in the immediate vicinity), having a private parking, attached to the store, is always one of the strong points that can determine its success: the simplest case to think about is "weekly shopping": which supermarket would be successful without parking? How would customers be able to carry their purchases if there was no possibility to park in the immediacy? Another important case is that of a fast food restaurant: if it aspires to make large numbers, it cannot be located in the absence of a car park or pedestrian zone (with a high traffic) because its model especially leverages on the convenience of people.

BAR-STAGING

From a general overview, we defined bar- staginqas a "less invasive intervention" than the total renovation, but equally effective: this in fact will not concern so much the room itself (intended as property), but rather the activity that takes place at the interior with a repositioning or change of furniture, colors, lights and perhaps the redistribution of the main points of attention to the public. Clearly, this intervention must observe stylistic and balance rules that only a professional or a very experienced person can give him: it is very frequent to see how the do it yourselfnfects inexperienced investors, who many times do not follow any logical canon and reproduce environments absolutely lacking in personality and consistency. It is a bit like when you take photos at a wedding: no matter how advanced the technology has been in recent years, you still pay a professional for large amounts, because you immortalize those moments: it is normal, that being an unrepeatable moment, you don't want to make a mistake, and you know perfectly well that these can produce hundreds of shots of remarkable quality, to the detriment of those who, with the do it yourself, could take a dozen really good photos. In fact, the professional has such training that he knows how to ignite the subject well, add certain details that detach, use some techniques (for example the lights) to accentuate certain atmospheres and organize the spaces in the way that the subjects stand out. The reprogramming intervention in bar-stagingis the same, because if done in a professional way it can absolutely make a store shine, in a way so superior that the practice of do-it-yourselfis absolutely noticeable "at the sight" of any profane, when making a comparison.

There is, however, one more step that differentiates a professional job in this field and it is the application of a change that reflects on corporate profitability: having already talked about the relevance of the counter in a bar, we take that example to highlight how much this distinctive element could influence profitability and also the geography and layout of the store. << We know that the bar counter is a cornerstone and we have thought of a hypothetical location; are we sure it is the correct one? >> The counter is perhaps the most distinctive character of this type of exercise and should always be located in a close-up view, completed by the back counter where you usually place bottles or glasses, or use it as a decoration. If we think of a rectangular-shaped shop, it is not the same thing to place it at the bottom, rather than at the beginning, rather than frontally or sideways: they are absolutely decisive and difficult decisions for an inexperienced person, because he would lose too far of importance and would be difficult to reach in certain types of night bars, irreparably lowering the volume of sales. Too close to the entrance could be a dramatic aesthetic solution and not entice you to enter the main hall, which would always appear a dark and distant place. << And if we put it in the middle of an island? And if we talk it straight from the side? >> Any decision will change the economic result of this company for better or for worse because the main product of this type works in this area. The do it yourselfin these cases could be lethal, because we tend to think only of the aesthetic sense and not of the practicality of the work or the profitability of the shop. There are also other criteria to be taken into account, to avoid seeing unpleasant situations, such as "a counter near the bathrooms" (where even smells or embarrassing situations are suffered at sight), or too far from the kitchen, which implies more personal and less control. Then we want to talk about the choice of whether to put or not to put stools that determines the type of clientele you will have? When the customer "eats and drinks on the counter" it is clear that there is work to be done in a different system than the classic table service. Let's talk about the color or the materials? Apart from an aesthetic criterion, we should evaluate the cost and durability of one of the main actors of this activity.

We could continue for hours talking about every single detail of a counter, and you think we are only at the beginning because then we have tables and chairs to discuss other hours, mezzanine or separate room, open kitchen or not, classic service, self-service or table service with show. Entry of a certain type rather than another. Terrace. Lights. Decorations, etc ... for each element we could spend hours discussing: however the main concept is only **<< each choice in a commercial premises is directly reflected on the turnover >>**, because it can make the tasks more or less easy to carry out, or it can make a place more or less pleasant and attractive. This does not mean that a perfectly set bar necessarily functions, because subsequently personal and managerial factors of the various entrepreneurs come into play, but surely, setting it up incorrectly is like starting with a handicap in an obstacle course.

<< The practicality added to an excellent aesthetic result and the optimization of the revenues through the organization of the spaces >>: this is what is what I have called bar-staging.

The novice investor almost always thinks only of aesthetics, and in most cases (not being a professional in this matter, dazzled perhaps by good ideas), he does not have the competence to develop and execute them correctly. The result is often called monotony with fairly standard and uninteresting rooms; even worse when they are not very functional. Think of those who have had in the past (today there are stricter regulations and certain things are not practicable), << the brilliant idea of placing a restaurant kitchen in the underground warehouse >> or upstairs, simply with the aim of increasing the number of tables by a few units. Space is undoubtedly very important, and the more tables you have, the more potential collections you can express. But can you imagine the inconvenience of such a solution and all the consequences it entails? Mind you, there are certain situations where it is necessary, especially in the city in old or small places where solutions must be invented, but being able to choose this is one of the typical solutions that "will make you lose money" because they will probably require more staff or the installation of a freight elevator, never solving the problem of practicality and slowing down the service offered.

There is nothing randomly located in a commercial space, not even the details that seem more insignificant.

Furniture and decoration are also not secondary: have you ever entered a place that aesthetically has an appearance and then once inside, feel completely out of context? Contradictions. The inexperienced entrepreneur often moves in this way: abuse of the do it yourself and then when he sees that the results do not arrive, he begins to listen to all the voices: < < why don't you add this? > >, < < why don't you change the other? > >: its trajectory therefore passes from “having mounted a monotonous room” to converting it into a “nonsense room” because it adds and changes details or objects (very often also good and expensive), which however is not they marry with each other, until you get to a non-homogeneous mix or jumble style disused objects, put at random (for the record there are rooms in this style, but they are absolutely studied: every object or thing "put at random", in reality is not 'not at all, because' everything follows rules and a coherence of style and design).

What is meant by this argument? That setting up a commercial space so that it is ready to host an activity is not at all a question that can be "done well", because every mistake affects work and entrances. Activities already involve many risks and many variables by nature: why add a problem? Just to save something or for an eagernessto lead? There are experts in what we have called bar-staging if we speak only of aesthetic criteria, for example, a home- staging professional or a good decorator or general architect can design the room without any problem. With respect to the unskilled investor without experience, surely at least it would be nice: and in fact **it is the error that many commit**, because they stop halfway: there are beautiful bars certainly designed by a professional who, however, normally dedicates himself to the market residential: for multiple reasons the result can be absolutely pleasant, but with enormous problems from the point of view of corporate life: beauty is not the only determining factor. So to get a superior result you would have to contract a professional bar-staging or **remodeling of a commercial premises** (therefore you are a decorator or an architect but who are purely trained in the commercial field), but here we are already in the field of "rare goods" because few have the skills to do such a job. You should certainly have drawing experience, to organize the spaces, but also experience of the type of business to be carried out and commercial marketing experience and many other types of experience. I personally, for example, have all the skills and experience necessary to perform a job of this type, given my professional trajectory, but only in the field of catering or leisure premises; for example, if I had to do it in a supermarket I would not feel comfortable, because apart from the aesthetic criteria, I do not know that type of activity and therefore I would not know how to optimize it: for this reason my "specialty" and my advice I only offer in the theme in which I have specific skills: that is, leisure and food and beverage venues.

Large companies, for example, have their own team that only deals with setting up one store after another. We also think, for example, of franchises which can be very large (or small) stores, in any case, replicated in many different places while maintaining the same distinctive features, the same aesthetic and structuring rules depending on the original design of the parent company, adapted to the technical limits of the property being furnished. They even have parameters, so tight that many times they discriminate certain areas by location, property characteristics and limitations (the parent company refuses to proceed with the operation often occurs). Normally smaller companies solve the problem of a professional decoration of a room, **with a mixture of figures** and a union of intent: the owner dictates the guidelines and explains what type of business he intends to set up; then there is an architect or decorator who takes care of the aesthetic part; if you are not forward-looking, the part of ductility and functionality linked to the organization of work remains a bit uncovered, something that is compensated with time and experience, or that should be entrusted to a professional third party, who is dedicated exclusively to that.

SCALAR INVESTMENTS

The truth is that there are many inexperienced investors: but in other cases, we find entrepreneurs who are very prepared and have had such good results that they are able to scale their business quickly. We have already talked about franchisingas the most intuitive system to reproduce what has been successful in a store, reproposed in a sane way in other locations. This is the most linear model of **scaling** a commercial **investment.** We think of hotel chains rather than supermarkets: once the first is assembled and produces high yields, the easiest thing to do is to replicate the same model at a distance of non-competition, thus minimizing risks, because it is adopted a winning project, and trying to control the territory: these are the first two steps to build a network of sales outlets and therefore dominate the market with your own brand. Among other things, there is also a tax issue to be analyzed: we all know that the first two years of an activity are customary that they result in losses due to the start up due to market resistance and due to the amortization of the investment that weighs on the budget: in a nutshell you pay duty to be in the beginning. But then if all goes well, breakeven points are reached and then the first profits appear. Without the spirit of offending anyone, no entrepreneur likes to pay too many taxes and when a company begins to produce a lot of profits, an investor must ask himself whether it is better to pay taxes (which would be a dry expense) or to reinvest. It could reinvest in the same starting activity and renew itself, but that I took for granted in the analysis, as normal practice to keep a store updated. The other chancehe has is to invest in another property or another business: he would therefore reduce the taxation because in this case it would be a matter of putting the new operation at "cost", and his profits would be zeroed in the financial statements. This practice is totally legal and is not at all a way to get around taxes; think of a supermarket that reinvests to open another: it will surely put the operation at cost and therefore will not pay taxes on the previous initiative. Why do the institutions allow him such an operation? Think for example of how many jobs this operation generates and how much additional economic activity. In turn, these factors lead to new taxes or a new reversal, if there are new budget profits, and so on. It is clear that the system is correctly assembled to promote entrepreneurial activity, work and economic life, with all the benefits that result from a positive activity.

There is however another system of doing business and "it is not replicating the winning model", but on the contrary **differentiating**, to have control over the whole of a sector, rather than to diversify the risks, rather than for the convenience of market: it is not unusual for some famous brands of specific products to start producing something different or that has nothing to do with the original product; I am reminded of the example in the Yamaha brand for example, a very famous manufacturer of motorcycles of all types. Perhaps not everyone knows that to scale their investment, for example, the same brand also produces other things, such as engines for boats, which have little to do with street bikes. The reasonthat moves this is the same that we have just explained about taxes and re-investment, but in this case the way is to differentiate the product. As for commercial properties, the contextualization could be exemplified in this paradox: << I am the owner of a very famous coffee shop and I have great profits: what do I do? >>: one of the possible ways would be to open another identical coffee shop in another location; but why not think of a business lunch restaurant instead? And so we move on to "control" the market in a wider range of time and with a clientele with superior economic capabilities. If there were further profits from the two initiatives undertaken, and you wanted to optimize your revenues, by leveraging marketing, you could expand the restaurant's activity and convert it also for evening work, where a higher price policy is applied. But it's not over: on another property, always using the profits of the assets, you can decide, in the end to even invest in a disco. With such diverse and independent activities, but belonging absolutely to the same niche (food and beverage and leisure) and good marketing, you can absolutely "control" a good portion of the public, loyal and of large numbers, because the market in that sector is being dominated with contiguous operations with each other: paradoxically a customer could spend a day of 24 hours in the companies described, sometimes even without even knowing who the property is. 'Subsequently, from this customer base, through the knowledge, a virtuous circle of customer turnover and all that will follow will be generated. In a nutshell, in the "commercial" there is no limit to the scalability of the business: the only detail is that you have to be truly prepared in your job, meet a truly productive system and then organize to reproduce it better than the competition.

marketing must convert and sell in the long run

CHAPTER 3: MARKETING FOR COMPANIES

DIFFERENCE BETWEEN MARKETING AND ADVERTISING

These two concepts are often confused with each other as if they were a synonym, but in reality they are to be considered "each other's container". Marketing not only includes advertising, but it is all **<< a set of actions and plans through the qualification of a result >>**, which in most cases connected << the increase in the value of a brand or brand >> (with economic consequences for the reference company).

The inexperienced entrepreneur translates it, trivializing it, often with << buy an infinite number of advertising products>>, or double ads and spots, because he mistakenly thinks that this means "do more marketing"this definition is wrong, because << marketing is only one>> and has no quantity (advertising is measured in quantity, marketing is not). It is a unique project which, through studied and varied actions, linked together, generate a result.

Let's take some very intuitive practical examples: << rate 20 radio and television announcements and updates increased to 100 is marketing medium? >> Sincerely, if these are the last words of the discussion, the answer is negative: this simply made of advertising costs on average, which in the short term can also assume a result, because it is statistically true that more announcements are made and you have more chances to be seen (what I am using is a very simplified model because we should also discuss the quality of these ads and where they are off It is therefore called **"advertising" << the act of increasing visibility >>** through actions, without there necessarily being an overall strategy other than the "purpose of directly increasing sales": it is possible, if incisive, to intervene in increase liquidity in the short term, but in the long run its benefits are difficult to measure. Advertising makes sense when you promote something in concrete, for example an event or a novelty, and you want to get this information as quickly as possible to a large number of possible users.

Let's take the case of an entertainment room: the advertising result is measurable when, through our announcements, many people will gather at a concert; in this case its effectiveness is proven. However, once the concert is over, its function will be practically exhausted and therefore it may have no effect on the future: it should therefore be counted as a cost, necessary to organize that event. When proceeding with the analysis of the costs of this action, it will be necessary to see if it was worth it or not. On the contrary, on the other hand, the strategy of "making live music concerts" can be considered a marketing strategy for this type of exercise: it is probably insufficient for the needs of an entertainment company to function, but if it is combined with other long period (which we will see later), can be absolutely successful. So where does it differ from advertising? Simple: advertising is the means by which to organize an event, but the fact of building a history of events and of continuously recycling people in that place is a marketing action: the aim of making music thus becomes an opportunity to attract an audience that then stations, spends and has fun and then in turn attracts other people for the next event. All marketing choices involve costs, but which are aimed at forming a general plan that must **lead to increase the company's turnover and brand value.** Now it is easy to understand how marketing is actually the "instigator" of an action, and advertising is only a "performer", that is, a mere tool (among other things, not the only one), to achieve it, but everything according to well studied logics in advance.

MARKETING POST COVID-19

Knowing how strategies will evolve following such large changes is very difficult; what can be hypothesized is that the systems will change but not the substance and the logics that have always guided the winning business choices from the period of the "industrial revolution" onwards.

Let's try to imagine how markets change and consequently marketing in a post-virus period. Clearly our attention will be mainly focused on real estate investments and commercial activities.

<< I will not go on to tell you about the Corona-virus as such, because unfortunately we have all experienced the period of this world pandemic that has just affected us and that has changed our lives, forcing us to take refuge in the house to escape them, but hopelessly blocking the direct economic system of different countries (indirectly affecting the entire world economy as a result). We all already know where it was born and how it spread, we know the numbers of the victims and the limiting measures that we had to take, but we don't know exactly the numbers of the economic damage yet: we may perhaps have a personal idea, which varies from company to company a company, according to what was invoiced in 2019 and will not be invoiced in 2020, but the consequences of all this will not be limited to 2020 alone and exactly it is difficult today to estimate how much it will affect the following years.

Do you wonder this consideration? Perhaps someone had deluded themselves that with a few months of isolation all this would pass and it could be cataloged as a bad memory to be forgotten as soon as possible. Unfortunately it will not be so and even if they are only theories, I will try to explain them to you in the most practical way possible, through examples, so that everyone can ask their own questions. "Questions": yes, because no one is currently able to give absolute answers; one can only make assumptions.

What is certain is that nothing will be the same as before, because the contemporary world has found itself vulnerable to something that not even Bin Laden and his terrorist organization had come to do: in 2011, in fact, the terrorist acts had made the most supportive and united world, strengthened the desire to unite and collaborate to overcome what had been a vile attack. It was almost as if terrorism had been defeated, apart from that by the US military, by itself, as it brought about the union under the flag of the United Nations, with an unimaginable sense and desire for freedom and pro-positivity: the terrorists' followers had frightened, but they had certainly not blocked the world: the world instead blocked it covid-19 nine years later. In fact, this bizarre virus, underestimated by all, has gone quite hidden for months, disguising itself with strange episodes classified then as simple "pneumonia" in the worst cases or spreading among the asymptomatic. He was not known, and therefore nobody feared him, and at the beginning he positioned himself strategically, to then appear officially in China and subsequently in Germany with the patient or European; but not officially he was already around the world, probably from the second half of 2019, sly, silent. Then when the "bubble" exploded and the numbers collapsed, this bizarre enemy was given name and surname, and then the fear began, above all because we discovered that we could not face it, neither from a medical point of view (no vaccine), nor were we ready with the facilities and numbers to deal with it from the point of view of the health emergency, with the various national systems overloadedin a few weeks. This time the enemy had hit his target: not only the direct victims, but all the consequences: fear outside the front doorTo demonstrate the weakness of an entire nation, even of many countries. And above all, to separate, given that it was one of the few wars in which the peoples, after reaching stability, felt more divided than ever: the various nations did not react in a uniform form, but in drops, they implemented very different in timing and reactions. There was solidarity and it is true, but late and in most cases not very effective.

People have reduced themselves to locking themselves up frightened (and not understanding) in their homes, without even having often embraced a family member. It was one of the few wars that divided "before, during and after", also because << loving each other in that moment hurt ", that is, you had to separate and distance yourself to stay safe: any contact could have been risky. Months of this psychological and media massacre that will change the way we perceive life forever. Unfortunately, those who will surely constitute the most significant legacy will not be good intentions, easy to forget in a few months, but the economic and social consequences of the thing >>.

- **HOW THE REAL ESTATE MARKET CHANGES FROM 2020 ONLY** << At the end of 2019 I was going to record my recurring videos of updates on the situation of the real estate market in my area of competence, and well in advance I highlighted how much the forecasts of the following year would have been clearly alarming, predicting and anticipating a real estate crisis at the end of 2020: probably, I was wrong, but only because I was optimistic, I could not know of the virus that inexorably did nothing but anticipate the steps that would have occurred anyway for other reasons: the already mentioned Brexit, tour operator crisis, new Middle East spotlight and holiday home inflation. I therefore expected the approach of an economic crisis (and of a real estate reflex) that would lead to the devaluation of the properties within a year, and first of althose less positioned or distinct. As well, we are all clear by now, this process is already underway and everything is taking place very quickly. The peculiarity of this crisis is that it will have gone from a final of the year 2019, with very high prices to a beginning of 2020 with prices in sharp fall: all in the space of a few months and without notice. This in the residential field, where however there will be differences for very unique properties or for particularly interesting areas; it will probably be a catastrophe for commercial activities, of which a good part had to make drastic decisions, such as "closing its doors" or selling, perhaps at a very devalued price, in a hurry.

In the future, there will probably be a kind of **natural selection,** where those who do not have a certain professionalism or economic strength are destined to disappear from the market. In a sense, not all evils come to harm because this will lead, in the long run, to higher average quality and less "inflation", but during this change there is always someone worthy who unfortunately cannot "stay on your feet "(and someone who is less deserving than with artifices or economic solidity resists and therefore follows the best).

The important issue will therefore soon be that of liquidity. How is this reflected on investments? The most obvious consequence is the lowering of prices on sales, but there is also to be taken into account that prices also go down because there are fewer people with the opportunity to buy. In reality, the market will return to being a market of "buyers" (that is, where the buyer is holding the negotiations), because there are already many investors who were organizing and were not moving, waiting for the favorable market swing to buy. as soon as the prices were more accessible. In fact, in recent years there had been a fairly widespread arrogance on the part of the owners in fixing the values of their properties, and the good investor had stopped buying, "letting buy" only private individuals, who had personal interests, rather than contingent needs, and they certainly could not wait years for a business cycle to change. So to think that there are no buyers is wrong, but now **the type of buyer will change:** be careful, however, not to be fooled by the "myth of the investor". Many times we have heard opinions of sellers who defined their properties or businesses as << perfect for an investor >>, often supported only by their personal desire or interest to believe in this thing. Investor does not mean "dumb". Quite the opposite! The veteran investor, for example, is the exact antipode of the owner, that is to say, through his communication, that << everything is worth less, really, than the value that is being attributed to him >>. So on the one hand the owner has a tendency to swell; on the other, the aggressive investor has a tendency to demonstrate that it is worth much less in the market. How can owners ever hope in vain for investors as saviors of the homeland? The reality is that they are investment professionals and are not used to buying off the market.

<< Sometimes I have been offered marketing assignments, for ancient buildings, at a price that we define in this example as 100. The goal that according to the owner I should have found was "an investor", because a private individual could not afford that outlay the first thing you do in these cases, look on the agenda for the first 5 numbers of the most important investors in the city and start calling. Unfortunately, often the answer is << Thanks, but I'm not interested, because I'm selling "the new one at 110", and therefore it costs too much. In fact, I would buy what you offer me, in a price between 50-60 because maybe it is worth 70. So considering all the expenses, at this price you propose is uneconomical >>. It is quite obvious that I refuse regardless of assignments of this type just after having informed the owner of responses of this type (and having seen that his reaction is absurd: << then let's try to lower it to 95 >>. << But if it is 70?! >>). I hope

it is quite clear that for this type of owner, **the investor will never be a resource**, just as this property will never be purchased by an investor (and probably under these conditions not even by a private individual), because it is out of the market.

So I'm painting a very problematic scenario, where there will be an absolute need for a change of mind-set by the owners and responsibility by the buyers: the former will necessarily have to adapt to the market, unless they decide and can afford to wait a new economic cycle in a few years, and the latter will not have to "pull the rope too much" and present absurd offers. From the balance of the two positions, the real estate system will return to turn and produce, and surprisingly it could be one of the first to recover, at least in the residential area in certain geographical areas. Everything therefore depends on the mind-set and the balance between supply and demand: the faster the adaptation to the new market, the faster the transactions will return >>.

- **SOCIAL AND ECONOMIC CHANGES**<< I see that the paralysis of the real estate system is therefore not expected, more simply a change, on the other hand a radical change in the uses and customs of people and the consequent economic shift of wealth by sectors is very certain.

Social and economic changes sectors. As we learned in the letter written by covid-19, this experience will change certain systems and ways of thinking, and above all it will concern entrepreneurship and the way of thinking about corporate life. Perhaps the real function of the virus, in the end, will be to really bring us into the XXI century, because until now everything had remained exactly the same as the XX century, with a slow and inexorable expiration of products and service in general. Is this the occasion for a real economic-industrial revolution?

The first effects of this experience have been seen in commerce and services. As the first activities were blocked by the restrictive decrees, they closed the physical store and organized or strengthened an existing online trade Obviously, bars, for example, cannot prepare us acocktail online nor offer us aggregation and fun; but apart from these cases, let's think about the marketing of clothes, housewares, products in general, and food products themselves (many people have started to request more supermarket home service for fear of going out to buy firsthand): previously only a small niche used these online servicesin this sense, but with limited confinement, for months, they have become more and more accustomed to searching the internet for a product and to request it for shipping. In this sense, it is plausible to think that companies of this type, for the future, will further strengthen this branch, and this could also change the logic of the stores, which have always worked until yesterday. It is quite obvious and obvious that there will therefore be a lot of changes from an organizational and social point of view, because people will get used to different things to meet their needs, and of this the market will have absolutely everything in mind. In the real estate market, therefore, the valuations will change, certainly also the strategies in the commercial field, which will determine new rules: now more than ever it will be necessary to look to the future, because another type of game is played >>.

- **RESIDENTIAL MARKET: WHAT CHANGES**<< The property has always had a fairly important and clear intrinsic value since the earliest times. Remember in the old Westwhen colonies and colonies of people went in search of luck. I am not talking about speculative and random search for gold, but about a more solid and secure form of investment or "land". This example means how ephemeral certain and even risky investments are, in spite of others who are absolutely always functional and with low probability of risk: << **a house is always a house**, it is worth a lot or it loses value, it will always be worth something> >, and by holding the property it can be used for different uses:

- PERSONAL USE: we take into account that everyone needs a home, **used to reside and live**. The house can be "owned" or "long term rent". An interesting assessment to make is that paradoxically we could say that in Europe, or in the United States, << there are more houses than families >>.

In this case, the scenario will remain almost constant even today, because everyone will continue to need "a roof"; however, there may be a redistribution following covid-19.

- PROFITABLE USE: following the reasoning above, the owners, who can instead afford to count with significant savings and liquidity, taking advantage of the opportunities of the moment, have acquired and are acquiring more than one property and if sometimes this is used as second residence (for pleasure) or to carry out its commercial or industrial activity, in other cases the purpose is to invest to rent to a third party. In the case of the lease, therefore, we can say that the property was purchased in order to produce capital. These capitals would be "proceeds from long, medium or short term leases depending on the policies adopted by the owner. By defining **the long term as "stable typology",** the medium term as an "innovation", interesting to monitor, and the short term as "speculative" and following trends, we can assume that in the post

Corona-virus it will continue and will be recommended "l 'long term rent".

- NO USE: I will surprise you by talking about this category because it is very interesting. << Who tells you that all properties serve some function? >>. They could only exist as a result of unplanned circumstances and be completely superfluous or even annoying (if we think that they must be maintained by paying taxes and maintenance to own them, without perhaps making use of them). We talk about wrong investments for example, never completed or unfinished, which therefore are not even in a condition to be rented, or we think about the inherited properties: the covid-19 or life in general, leave traces in 2020 of many deaths; many of these people were owners and therefore their heirs could either be new owners (and move from the condition of rent to that of having a first home) or they could simply inherit properties in unexpected form of which they do not know objectively what to do with them. These properties will be real **market opportunities**, in many cases because, once the emotional barrier is overcome, if careful commercial evaluations are made, there will be a good sales motivation and therefore market-compliant prices: in these conditions, many potential investors will want to win them for personal or investment purposes. It is difficult, although unfortunately sometimes it happens, to think that good properties remain unused to ruin inexorably over time: a wise owner will have to think how to use that capital before it devalues, because time deteriorates without remedy >>.

• **COMMERCIAL MARKET: WHAT CHANGES** << In this field, total uncertainty reigns, because the scale of what has happened is still to be measured. We previously mentioned a sort of natural selection, **where the best or those with the most financial resources will survive**, and also a sort of change in the structuring of certain points of sale and consequently of the type of property: if, for example, it took hold scale the automated selection and delivery of supermarket shoppingit is reasonable to think that small shops would suffer the latest lethal blow, and that food companies would dive into huge warehouses and warehouses organizing Amazonstyle deliveries, instead of aiming for management of expensive stores located in strategic places. Natural selection and change of concept are in progress, therefore the effects of these changes cannot yet be predicted. However, we have also mentioned an old and expensive sector, which however cannot be expressed with today's technologies and cannot be performed in virtual form, because it has to do with the aggregation and production of "something done at the moment"; if you think about it, it is really the only thing that cannot have a corresponding virtual version. In fact, even if it is not the same, in extreme conditions you can see a football game virtually, or order any product and service, or make meetings and have friends and even a virtual girlfriend: but you will never "go to the bar virtually ". The food & beveragesector is not a type of trade that can be replicated in virtual form. Surely therefore, if on the one hand the classic shop risks disappearing due to the social changes or habits that people, restaurants, bars and hotels would assume, as "aggregation sellers and emotions" and a product that can only be used in a three-dimensional way "Live", they will continue their existence, albeit undergoing an important inflection of the numbers for the reasons already explained. However, there will also be an important exchange of sellers here who, due to the change in customer habits or to the accounts which are no longer favorable, will decide to sell, creating important market opportunities, in positions or situations that until some time before were unthinkable. The real "sharks" (expert investors), should be ready now with their capital to position themselves and take advantage of these market opportunities.

But what is the identikit of this type of investor?

It is absolutely a very expert and abundant profile, because the first thing that he will have very clear is that he will not start earning in the short term, but his is an investment over time: **he is only buying a good position at an advantageous price**, but it is very likely that, if he wants to assemble an activity today, he will have difficulties like everyone else, unless he again resorts to economic resources to build and position an activity as market leader The beginner investor then? Someone from this other group will certainly move equally, even in unfavorable conditions, and will probably burn especially if they do not have specific skills in the business and economic reserves to deal with times of depression. All economic cycles offer market opportunities: the theme is "knowing how to read the score in advance" and moving accordingly >>.

CORONA VIRUS SEEN AS "GREAT MARKETING GENIUS"

Let's pretend for a moment that this strange enemy isn't completely against us, and let's study it as an economic example to steal its secrets in a totally neutral and selfless way.

Seen in this light, unconsciously covid-19, if we compared it to a company that wants to enter the market, it has moved with an absolutely unique and unrepeatable intelligence and strategy. Let's think about how silent he remained until the first days of 2020. He had organized himself and had been gathering all his forces probably for at least six previous months, without making any noise, << hiding and dressing himself with other names >> (when we thought it was a flu or in the worst case pneumonia). It was probably already present all over the world then, with the unconscious and often asymptomatic people, and it was multiplying, expanding and above all **positioning itself:** positioning is very important in an economic model, because it can discriminate the size, the times and the possibility to be successful. In the case of the virus, the positioning was intelligent and silent, and when he was now ready to launch his attack, he did it << from the best location, with the greatest possible strength, with speed, with the surprise effect, breaking the competition (ie leaving the various health services helpless) >> and rapidly consolidating itself as a reality that has dominated the market, that is our lives. In fact, when the right moment arrived, not only did he make himself known, but he also went to a more aggressive phase: he came to the " boom", where he routed everyone and fulfilled his purposes.

This, for example, is also a case of so-called << occult marketing >>, that is, without advertising. Advertising had to be done by the man later to understand what was happening: but the virus itself embarked on a perfect marketing strategy that quickly made it reach its goal.

I imagine that it is not exactly the most pleasant example I could use, but it certainly has an impact and can clearly explain how we should move in the market. Different strategies can be implemented (aimed at attracting attention such as advertising or occult as in the case explained), but the aim is always the same: the company must grow and expand according to a project and strategies well outlined and arrived at a certain point it has to "explode" to compete at full speed in the market. On the contrary, if you cannot reproduce this growth model, it is inexorably destined to decline because you are probably moving with inadequate marketing logic.

MARKETING ACTIONS IN COMMERCIAL ACTIVITIES

Different strategies can be implemented, but the winning point from which world and world is to vary the way or ways of proposing oneself, therefore to advertise and promote, while maintaining coherence in the strategy and direction, in the intrinsic characteristics of a given company, , with the aim of being able to correctly represent the main characteristics of the same and its proposal. So, meaning marketing as << **a set of strategies applied to achieve a predetermined purpose** >>, we will now analyze in general the fundamental characteristics of this type of planning, and then we will go on to list and explain the most suitable techniques for promoting in the 21st century, updated for technology and incisiveness.

It should be noted that it is not said that identical marketing actions produce the same results, discriminating over time, in the product and by the different companies. Often the non-expert eye does not understand why a strategy works for certain categories and for others not, and above all many times emulation is used as a "way out" to solve problems: it is in fact common sense that << a something that works very well for someone it could also work for others >>, but the opposite is also true, because it depends on the difference from the activities, each action has a different incisiveness according to certain ad hoc criteria.

Taking a concrete example in the food and beverage sector, it is not the same thing to promote a disco rather than a restaurant for business lunches: in the first case the goal is to sell "fun", therefore you have to create campaigns where the taste is enhanced to be together celebrating, transgression, movement, events; in the second case we need to be more concrete, quick and comfortable, because the goal is << to make it clear that good quality production is made at a fair price >>, which is the only thing that the recipients of that message are looking for : all the other factors that are secondary and typical of other types of restaurants, where people meet for pleasure and for the taste of eating and not purely for a need.

So setting up a wrong and not targeted marketing campaign on the objectives that are appropriate for your business is a waste of time and resources, therefore a cost. Also in this case there is a widespread "do it yourself" where many owners (apart from feeling decorators, entrepreneurs, cooks etc ... and excel in all these disciplines) even feel marketing experts: almost always these subjects simply end up by buying some random advertisements, certainly not implementing marketing policies! Remember that those who have been practicing in a certain business sector for many years probably know how to do all these things fairly well and have the experience to be able to at least distinguish the incisive actions from the lesser ones; but certainly those who do not have at least 15-20 years of experience, how can they think that it is so easy to replace a professional, from any of these fields, who always and only exercises his own subject and has repeated it in an innumerable number of occasions and in different contexts? Let's think about how vain, in the example taken to the extreme, could be to advertise "the convenience or speed of execution of cocktails" in a disco; with inverted parts, it is equally harmful to advertise the "great agglomeration of people and fun" in a business restaurant: even counterproductive therefore, in the second case where people are looking for something simple and disconnect a few minutes from work. Consistency, balance and clarity are essential in marketing, exactly as they were when we defined Bar- staging(harmony of message and elements): in fact, I consider the point of salein marketing as an integral or fundamental part. But when you make the wrong advertisement at a store, it can lead to nothing or even a negative result. Think of a luxury restaurant for example, which has a certain level of customers, and has a high pro-medium price: why should it announce its activity in the "most popular newspaper in the city", if it does not work with large numbers, but with a niche of a certain social level? On the contrary, that niche of people, who would normally also pay a surcharge such as << taste of having something exclusive >>, could see this type of action as a decline or a downward path: it is the typical case in which even get to lose customers. It can be seen in this example, how a certain wrong line, too generalist, results in "mixing customers too much", that is, ruining their selection and uniqueness; in other cases there may be real changes in the type of user, and this of course can be conscious or unconscious, winning or absolutely losing, because at the mercy of events, and not instead the result of a strategy.

There is an old motto that says << in trade it is better that they speak badly rather than not speak >>. In a sense this was absolutely true in the 80s and 90s, but already with the new millennium and the internet (and subsequently with social networks) this concept has changed: before the comment, although negative it was dispersed and was considered totally random: rather than going as "anonymous", it was preferred to "be unpleasant", provided that people talked about a brand. This type of marketing action continues to be valid and very incisive for example in gossipor in the reality TVIndustry: it is the creation and projection of characters and situations, for which interest is created regardless of liking, because in any case it is created curiosity. However, already in the field of work and professionalism one must be very careful: with new technologies word of mouth is created artificially and can be a weapon in one's favor, but also give the coup de grace to any company, when negative . In fact today, almost all the large platforms dedicated to commerce, rather than to leisure in general, give anyone the opportunity to express themselves and therefore can tell the good and the bad of things, adding photos, comments and details, and thus creating media phenomena whereby << a place that is generally appreciated can become the best, while those who are not popular, can be completely sunk >>. In this case, if excellence cannot be achieved, it is better to go anonymously rather than poorly: from anonymity one could reprogram and start again; from widespread denigration, it is then necessary to reset everything, with an increase in costs and problems that cannot always be overcome.

In a world of "like"you therefore have the option << or not to get involved >> and to use the old commercial system (surely always a solid base, but not too competitive in certain fields nowadays), or get involved, but at that point you have to do it with the necessary investments and skills, in order not to have important negative repercussions. Once again, therefore, the "overturned concept" in business, so << it is not always true that those who spend less, really spend less >>.

Let's take a paradoxical example: today, we have all taken a plane in life. Why do you think they put two pilots for each plane plus the automatic pilot? The fairly simple answer is that << in an emergency, a beginner could hardly replace a pilot in something so delicate and technical >>. Professionalism is based on the fact that you pay a fee to someone to perform an action, which a layman would do with less quality, with more experience and a different management of unexpected events. So let's put ourselves in the perspective of being more critical with ourselves when we have a business and think sincerely << if we are spending a lot of money on simple advertising >> or if we are doing marketing research, because the costs can sometimes be similar, but the results certainly differ.

Clearly, even in marketing, it is necessary to distinguish who can help us express impact actions, in accordance with the type of company or goal we set ourselves: among the various professionals there are those who know how to deal with marketing in general, rather than others who know make certain specific and targeted actions on specific sectors. For example, in my personal experience, I as a real estate, I deal with marketing and marketing projects intended for the public "houses"; also expert in food and beverage and entertainment, I dedicate myself to the commercial activities of this sector; I would never dream of promoting marketing campaigns for a cosmetic industry, for example! The principles are obviously the same, but I would not have the knowledge of "how that type of work develops", nor of the strong points, nor of what exactly those specific customers want: let's say that I could do it well to half.' Just like those who do not really and deeply know the "bar" sector and use the "do it yourself" they can rarely or partially do well in promoting it. Using only 50% means "not optimizing a lot of potential" available. Think of a team game, if you were to pull from a rope: one team uses two arms, but the other uses only one; it seems quite obvious to me who will end up winning the game (regardless of who is the strongest or least), because there is one of the two teams that is not using its full potential.

In Spain, present throughout the online territory for consultancy (and available for live services only in certain territories, there is for example www.bares360.es with which I collaborate: this web page is the example of an agency strategic marketing for food and beverage and intrateinment companies, in the round: it offers all the most exclusive services for this type of sector, given the experience of its collaborators in this area. Newborn on the web, but made by people for years in this type business, ranging from the studied design of the venue, not only from an aesthetic point of view, but from the aforementioned functionality and optimization of spaces aimed at increasing revenues. We then move on to purely marketing services such as the creation of logos, advice on how to carry on web pages and social media, consultancy on company and personnel organization, event organization and much more. One of the most important branches, however, remains the sector of assistance for the sale of commercial activities or creation of companies to manage them: it is a very technical real estate niche but absolutely important for optimizing your investments; even in this section there is a course on << divestments of activities >> dedicated to real estate agents, which testifies to the need to provide "professional training" on these topics, with the aim of optimizing the work and entering all of them: these products (also the setting up of the store and the sale of the company) are important marketing actions and must be treated as such.

THOSE WHO DO NOT NEED MARKETING

This is a very hard and clear paragraph, where I would like to express my personal disappointment towards those who adhere to this "non-strategy", which is even worse in my personal ranking than those who "hurt marketing", but at least try.

Do not do marketing, it means not having a defined project aimed at achieving a result: that is, it means doing casual entrepreneurial activity, according to how it comes. It is quite evident that this does not agree with me, because if things are left "to chance" or follow a logic of taste, but not commercial, this can only produce a mediocre result. In response, therefore, to the issue we are analyzing, the casual, the inexperienced, or who would be better to change jobs before losing everything, do not do marketing. Of course, in life (unfortunately or fortunately) there are always exceptions, so even the most inept can sometimes achieve results, because kissed by luck and chance, or because it has significant economic resources that make up for other shortcomings. But in most cases, "non-control" or failure to plan is an it is an absolute source and the first sign of failure. There are instead subjects who boast or boast of not having to do marketing, because they have such a strong brand or a positioning that makes them unique and detached from the need to push.

We think of renowned and historic activities, which now automatically have a widespread word of mouth and therefore are totally free of interest in promotions. These realities are probably the only ones that can afford non-programming, because they live off their history's income, and therefore consider it more important to focus more on maintaining certain standards, rather than investing in growth. Admirable and respectable as a concept and absolutely truthful, even if they do not take into account one essential thing: time and change. These companies won't do marketing, but in the past their founder probably did it, and how! Thus they reached certain levels of excellence. We know, however, that the passage of time determines economic changes that are reflected in the industrial and commercial sphere, so it is not said that << what is good today also works tomorrow >>. It is quite plausible that these types of businesses are not concerned, at the present time, with applying marketing policies, but this obviously at the expense of any growth: over the years they will have to be ready when they have to change situations, for renew itself and apply policies aimed at relaunching its business to keep it competitive, in step with the times.ute source and first sign of failure.

There are instead subjects who boast or boast of not having to do marketing, because they have such a strong brand or a positioning that makes them unique and detached from the need to push. We think of renowned and historic activities, which now automatically have a widespread word of mouth and therefore are totally free of interest in promotions. These realities are probably the only ones that can afford non-programming, because they live off their history's income, and therefore consider it more important to focus more on maintaining certain standards, rather than investing in growth. Admirable and respectable as a concept and absolutely truthful, even if they do not take into account one essential thing: time and change. These companies won't do marketing, but in the past their founder probably did it, and how! Thus they reached certain levels of excellence. We know, however, that the passage of time determines economic changes that are reflected in the industrial and commercial sphere, so it is not said that << what is good today also works tomorrow >>. It is quite plausible that these types of businesses are not concerned, at the present time, with applying marketing policies, but this obviously at the expense of any growth: over the years they will have to be ready when they have to change situations, for renew itself and apply policies aimed at relaunching its business to keep it competitive, in step with the times.

MARKETING ACTIONS TO OPTIMIZE THE FOOD AND BEVERAGE SECTOR

As we said, marketing has basic rules that apply to all types of businesses, so the vast majority of what we will deal with now is widely applicable to other sectors: however I wanted to focus on my specialty and use my experience to talk about all the new technologies (and the classic system) available to companies, in this case of entertainment and catering: the new technologies are all those that apply since the advent of the internet, and therefore a lot has to do with the computer and a channeling of virtual means, aimed at increasing the value of the brand. The classic system is instead << all that series of systems that have always been used and that are old workhorses >>: a real solid base, which never expires from being important, but which if applied "alone", nowadays it may be insufficient to compete in the global world. The measure of all this also lies in the size of the market to which we refer: the more we talk about large markets, spaces and great competition, the more the need to differentiate and stand out is evident. In the small realities, however, the value of this whole study loses slightly strength at the expense of quality and interpersonal characteristics and empathy (which in any case never hurts to possess in any type of situation).

- **DIFFERENCES BETWEEN OLD SCHOOL AND NEW TECHNIQUES:** some of the dogmas of the old way of thinking was << being always present anyway >> and << the important thing is to make people talk about themselves >>. Claims also true, previously, but insufficient in 2020 because neither of them talks about programming. Maybe they could have been two good considerations at the advertising level, but today in any case they would be outdated, or better to integrate. In fact, not only must we be present, but we must choose the channel and be very competitive: the goal is to please and therefore project a perception of our business that attracts positive comments. It is a technological version of old school word of mouth, but the big news is that "people's opinions are in writing", easily available and accessible to everyone: they are called reviews. By now the largest platforms also use this system to characterize the product a little: especially in online shopping, where a person cannot see or touch with his hand, he often guides himself with the description of the product, with photos and videos and with comments from other people who have already purchased it. I state that personally I do not go crazy to buy based on the random opinion of others, and that I find it quite unpleasant when some friends < < choose where to go to eat pizza looking at who has more stars > >. I confess, however, that the system is absolutely valid, even if it has advantages and disadvantages:

- ADVANTAGES: Among the advantages, there is certainly transparency for the customer, so when a person sees all negative reviews he can reasonably think that he is looking at the announcement of something that has potential problems. Another advantage, always for the customer, is the peace of mind to buy when he sees evaluations of positive experiences, and which therefore gives him added security to do the same. Another advantage is that of in-depth description, where someone who has been able to have small problems (and then solved them) explains their path so that a third party can be conscious and decide what to do. The advantages are also for the seller: positive reviews almost always coincide with the increase in sales, and positive opinions are a great marketing action, which, in a chain, develops a positive word of mouth and a positive impression that is reflected on the brand Positive reviews also produce a replacement within the clientele of a company, and therefore a long-term growth, as well as the possibility of accessory sales (you were looking for an object, you mistakenly thought that that brand had it, but you discover others that interest you for other reasons, which you had not thought of): therefore the opportunity to diversify.

- DISADVANTAGES: when instead you do badly or have a bad marketing strategy, reviews can be a very unpleasant and annoying boomerang, which slows down growth, or even sinks the company in cases where this is not strong or to motivate them and to counter them or to be able to express such a high number of sales that they pass through without being perceived. In fact, in the case of many negative reviews, buyers will tend to curb their easy enthusiasm and deepen more. Sometimes they will give up. However, it is important to keep in mind that << all companies have negative reviews >>, even the most popular ones.

Let's take an example: could someone live now without "what's app"? It is the best mobile communication platform, the first in its history and the most widespread, capable of eliminating the use of ancient text messages, and has now become a must for almost everyone. Are there better applications? Maybe yes: they were born and there are several, but certainly less widespread and it will be very difficult for them to undermine this, as it continues to renew itself, strengthen its servers and grow. In fact one of the characteristics that belong to it are the absolute reliability of the program and the power of the servers. Other similar applications are perhaps more beautiful and nice, but not functional. Can you believe that "what's app", in reviews 1 to 5 of online stores, has a rating lower than 4? Incredible for something almost necessary first now, to communicate and work. Yet many negative reviews come, based on completely personal tastes and episodes. The disadvantage of a bad review is that of falling into the trap of the so-called "haters", that is, the discontents who sometimes exaggerate, leave their opinion in the comments. The comments, which can be both expressive and numerical to determine a rankingwill therefore depend on the fact that there are not too many negative reviews, which lower the average. This is why it is important nowadays to have a good marketing plan: there are few systems to counter negative reviews and depend on an accurate growth plan of your virtual image, which must have the possibility to counter them: technical arguments, in the case in which which are extended comments or the strength to disperse them having just as many positive ones, when there is a problem of evaluation. Think about the online market and how many times a seller prefers to refund their product, even when there are differences with the customer, when the opportunity to receive a negative review is feared: it could lose much more than the value it has sold us, if only they followed a couple of other negative reviews and lowered its reliability status. So you have to be very careful with marketing today, because unlike the old-fashioned word of mouth, it leaves a trace and directly and indirectly affects sales. In catering it is the same, raised to the nth degree! The old motto << people attracts people >> could be modernized with << positive reviews attract people >>, thinking of the various "tripadvisor", specific sites or even just the Google index, where everyone uses the same system.

What not everyone knows that there is "the trick", so there are systems designed to be reviewed, and even real "review professionals" who do it just like a job and are dedicated to opening special accounts for do what is a real job, but which if done well can launch one product at the expense of another. The techniques vary unlike the various portals, but the principle is the same: << start being nice and others on the same wavelength queue >>. Many businesses do not even realize they are wrong or that they are going wrong, because by not taking care of their virtual image, they do not even notice they have many haters. Was it easier and more genuine before, with the old system of working? Maybe, or maybe not: we mentioned advantages and disadvantages; what is certain is that the old systems, still very valid and milestones of commercial marketing, are not sufficient by themselves to compete at a high level.

- **MARKETING EVERGREENS** Still very present, especially in certain sectors, **flyersand signage** have always been two very powerful advertising vehicles. One arrives directly in people's mailboxes and can be differentiated in various formats such as flier (or booklet), business letter, private letter, etc ... It is undoubtedly always a powerful means, but has always had the obvious defect of high costs, due to of printing (even if digital printing has greatly reduced its prices today), but above all because of distribution, which is a job that can be done in a light and casual or professional way: the work done superficially is enough fast, and produces poor results for dispersion. In the case of a more expensive service with more guarantees, it is clear how much the costs may worsen; then we add the possibility that after such an important effort, the flyer may never reach the recipient's hands, as many buildings have a common "trash" for advertising (and I did not use the word trash at random!). The habit then of certain owners, even when leaflets were found in the mailbox, is to throw them in most cases without even reading them. So let's talk about an even worse case of not doing marketing: **<< think you have done it >>**, that is to say you have invested money and resources and seriously think you are doing something well, which instead is not so incisive. In large cities where the use of this technique in fact in past years was disproportionate, the incidence has dropped dramatically., Even if we record that it is always an old workhorse and if well implemented, with the right distribution, it is a evergreen.

The same goes for road signs for example. You have to differentiate yourself and certainly the road has always been one of the plausible places of visibility. This is also a workhorse, but certainly less incisive, in the presence of many other signs, because it is lost to the eye and sight. So it is important to do a study of << where it is profitable to place the signs >> in a strategic way according to the visibility and also according to the user you want to recall: << it seems a waste of resources to advertise women's beauty products in an industrial area, with mainly male density: net of the exceptions, there will never be numbers to pay back the investment, because the desired public is in other areas of the city >>. A very important example of signage is instead that of "repair or support" under the distinctive sign of a store. In cases where you approach the desired location, it is interesting to have indicators that warn you in advance and especially when you have a sign for location or technical limits, << hardly visible >>: it is absolutely necessary to consider investing in billboards in strategic positions and immediacy, which make up for this lack and enhance the store.

In the old school, we mention techniques relating to **newspapers, television and radio.** With the various differences in cost and type, they are always respectable evergreens, because many users access them daily. Unlike the first two vehicles, these are "placeable" and can be modulated on the type of customer (there are newspapers or radio for all age and social target groups). Or for example we think of TV with thematic channels, rather than with time slots: determining "when and how" therefore allows you to be more incisive and start skimming the majority of the desired audience. What I would like to highlight most is the incidence of local radio and television, which is absolutely important for a company. Think of the best restaurant in our city: what interest would it have to go on national television to advertise itself, and pay very high commissions? It could have only one narcissistic purpose, but from an economic point of view it would be totally too onerous and little incident. On the other hand, in local television, it would access practically all the desired users, i.e. that of its own city, and could discriminate the interest groups according to schedules and programming, because using sports, costumes and news services, this type of means of communication, with the its schedule, is very attractive for those who want to keep up to date on news related to their territory: this will also be the preferred audience to attract with our corporate marketing.

Another great classic is the posting on **buses and taxies** in large cities: it is a widespread and always current system, but which, depending on the number of reproductions or sizes, can be very expensive in terms of costs. and therefore the opportunity must be carefully considered before deciding to apply this type of policy, which I consider very aggressive and important.

We could go on for hours making other examples, but the concept is that the old school represents everything that has always been done in terms of visibility more than anything else physics, that is something that you can touch or move but that has always found in the big limit of the costs of production or service its great brake, in the past often generating exorbitant accounts under the budget item "advertising": for this reason, there was in the past among the entrepreneurs the widespread and perhaps then truthful opinion, that << advertising is not measurable >>, that is, it has to be done, but you never know what it really brings you! Modern marketing concepts, especially with the spread of advertising on the web, have radically changed this concept.

- **MARKETING 2020** The advent of the internet shocks the world since the beginning of the new millennium, but nobody at the beginning would have thought that we would have come so far when we installed the first modem years ago << which made whistles and gargles >> and was very slow at point to leave us desperate for minutes... waiting to see a normal website. Today with modern technologies, and super browsing speed, we watch films and programs live or recorded, we make video conferences and (consciously or unconsciously) we receive continuous marketing messages all day long by everyone: therefore the potential visibility of this action is absolutely constant and extremely powerful, considering that by now we have it on the computer at work all day and on the cell phone in the private sector, even at night. So the spreading and breaking down of borders is one of the great achievements of virtual marketing, capable of reaching indiscriminately everywhere and reaching anyone with well-applied strategies. Another of the important achievements concerns the reduction of costs: the internet is virtual, and therefore it does not require production and limits the service to a minimum. Even modern techniques allow the user himself to "self-manufacture" an ad and launch it, paying practically only a commission. Lately producing advertising has become so easy and cheap that it is within everyone's reach, so much so that one of the first disadvantages of this has been the loss of the desire to invest capital in advertising. We have therefore gone from the realization of expensive campaigns with billboards and magnificent initiatives, to admitting only free advertising for our company, trusting in the various facebook and similar applications (often totally free), with the conviction and the purpose that these actions are sufficient to promoting the business': in reality they don't even know each other very well (remember that commercial use is much more complex than private use) and it is often another example in which we think of advertising incisively, but we are just getting there to a small part of the market share, or to a few acquaintances and friends.

Indeed, one of the consequences of the popularity of the network is that anyone is online, privately or commercially, and therefore a series of related problems arise that are not always known. The first is technical, that is, the various social media applications allow the display of a free advertisement only to a certain number of users according to an algorithm: that is, they are excellent for organizing a private party for a few dozen people (use for to which they were expressly conceived), but to fill a stage they are insufficient if used in standard form. It is therefore necessary to apply certain techniques to make them more preforming and enter into the perspective of understanding that << the jump from super expensive advertising in the 90s to zero-cost advertising in 2015 is too large for a commercial activity >>.

We must continue to invest and have results and apply the correct actions of a targeted marketing aimed at optimizing revenues. In fact, only through investments and certain actions of an important quality, it is possible to stand out from the crowd. If everyone is on the internet, this means that you have to emerge and differentiate yourself from others, because obviously the daily attention has limits and the mind of the average user is constantly bombarded with messages all day and every day. We will now go into detail to see all the most important techniques, to highlight a company by using the new generation of virtual commercial marketing and proposing the updating of certain classic concepts readapted to 2020 with the updated version and the application of new technologies.

- **COMPANY LOGO:** everything must start with the logo. The logo is the expression of a brand, summarized in a drawing or an inscription. It must identify who we are and what we do, be attractive and captivating and must give a sense of continuity because it will appear in all the marketing actions we will do. It is a bit like the business card of the business, but in a virtual version applicable to everything: newspapers, television, internet stocks, signs, price list, even uniforms and corporate work tools. To the customer's eye, he will always identify the company, first reminding him that it exists and then why he should use it. The best logos are simple. They can be colored and absolutely must be original; sometimes there is the creation of surreal logos by companies of the highest order and level: in these cases, the virtual image that they will project is compromised.

- **SIGN OF THE POINT OF SALE** The sign characterizes the store and the message we address to the public about our product. The visibility is very important which not only depends on the size, but also and above all on the "visual field" of a customer with respect to the situation (in a pedestrian street where people move slowly, different techniques are applied, rather than on a sliding highway); to take into account also the night and day factor where new technologies absolutely help us both for a typical aesthetic taste, but also for the flexibility and increased visibility that they allow. It is always advisable to include the logo and a simple but impactful message and to use very simple characters that are not crowded together, because as we said earlier, the world now moves at such a speed that complex things often get lost in sight.
- **WEB PAGE:** Years ago, as soon as this novelty was introduced and cleared through customs, it was easy

enough to make companies understand that they had to have a page that talked about them in a widespread way, that explained their products and put them in contact with their users. There are different types of web pages, and I'm not talking about colors or graphics, where there is a whole art and special professionals, but I'm talking about types of use:

- ADVERTISING WEB PAGE: the classic example is that of the restaurant that publishes its menus location, a few photos and therefore wants a customer to find his page so that he can get information and be curious to visit the store.

- SUBSTITUTE WEB SITE OF THE POINT OF SALE: the most typical example is Amazon a giant of online commerce, where you can buy anything you would buy in a hypermarket, and in fact replaces it completely, except for the food sector (but they have the structure and the network to do it in the future: do you think that if there were new covid-19-style diseases, with all that it represented, they wouldn't think about managing a food sale? In any case, if not them, there are others of smaller size that they do and are empowering it).

- WEB CURRICULUM PAGE: practically it is a professional page where a professional or worker offers his own person and makes himself available for services. - PURE WEB PAGE: online activity page or online service. The most typical example are thematic pages dedicated to videos, for example: free of charge by advertising bannersor paid by subscription, they perform their function directly from their virtual platform. All these models and others are absolutely essential to carry out your business, but they all lack marketing: it is not enough to have a web page. Let's go back to the example of << believing you are doing an action >> which, however, is actually not incisive. A web page is of very little use if it is not easily encountered and nowadays finding things in the chaos of internet information is really complicated. Having a web page and then not applying certain actions to enhance it, is like having a restaurant located in a super secondary street that is very difficult to find. Clearly the potential audience changes. The first thing to explain is that therefore the web page must be indexed on search engines, through keywords and other marketing techniques that will increase its visibility. If people start to find it, and secondly to find it attractive, the visibility numbers will increase in algorithmic form because the various search engines always favor the best web pages, at the expense of the less searched ones. This is fundamental, because many times it is the fine line between success or failure. With different logics and algorithms, it is a bit like what happens with real estate portals when you put your house on sale: do you think it is important to remain visible at the top of the list of ads or is it the same to have a poorly indexed ad? The answer is that sometimes when it is very specific or very niche they find it anyway, perhaps with more effort, but it doesn't change much. But in matters of large numbers, a lot changes! In the same way, index your website and have it present in the first pages of the search engines enhances both the site itself and your company and therefore makes the marketing action undertaken effective.

Another discriminant is the content of the site. Again, I'm not just referring to aesthetic issues. I was the first to make the mistake of << wanting to put everything >> in the past many times. It is obvious that the online site of a technological e-commerce must put all its televisions, all its computers, all the household products that it holds, and the more things it does, the better it is: this is because it is selling a "product list". But in most cases the product is only one or they are few and when creating the site there is a tendency to write a lot, and therefore useful information is often lost. The web page must be easy and intuitive and present essential products and services. It must have simple but attractive graphics and must have cohesion with the physical store if there is one.

To make up for these shortcomings and also for the purpose of selling, the concept of **landing pages** has recently been introduced which are nothing more than other related web pages, which often refer to the main web page, but created specifically for the purpose of selling. In other words, since the website is very dispersed and must contain a lot of information, pages that are easier to index are launched which recall the main details, but which are graphically even more intuitive and minimalist, which have a clear message and which attract the customer. Maybe promoting a gift or with some absolutely commercial artifice. These obviously are indexed in turn in search engines through marketing techniques, but above all their use is becoming particularly interesting in the commercial application of social media, where attention is always undermined by too much information and there is a need for very simple impact.

- **SOCIAL MEDIA:** Similarly to the fact that everyone uses "what's app", everyone knows today what facebook, twitter, instagram and all the various social mediavariants on the market are, which differ in technology and potential audience. Social media are collectors of people who allow them to stay in touch with each other and interact virtually by writing texts, publishing photos and videos and with dozens of other more complex and varied functions depending on the genre. The first, most famous and known is Facebook, which is now present in practically all our homes. It was undoubtedly one of the greatest innovations of the past twenty years because it improved communication and allowed us to break down social barriers, which until a few years ago seemed insurmountable. It is evident that, as in everything, on the other hand, it has also brought many problems, such as the birth of the famous "fake news," that is, the fake, fictional, distorted news, or real interpersonal conflicts, for the most varied reasons. On the other hand, however, it was also a very powerful commercial vehicle because those who understood in time the application and importance of these advertising media, studied the algorithm and understood how to optimize marketing campaigns in order to reach more people: the same announcement can reach only 1000 people instead of one hundred thousand depending on the policies adopted. Unfortunately, in this case the do it yourselfhas always had the perception of reaching everywhere in the world (and potentially it is because there really are no barriers), but the creators of the algorithm, once seen the widespread expansion of the platform, they had to put some restrictions, understanding first that for example << who organized a popular concert in the center of Madrid, it was useless that it was visible in New York >> and in a more restrictive form, that it was visible even in the south of Spain it is wasted.

Potentially a New Yorker, for his part, can always search and find this event, exactly like all the events published in the world, in any location they are, however, unless he has a direct relationship with the organizer or an acquaintance , or is not interested in that niche, in theory "does not interest him" and therefore it is right that he does not see it. (this is the sense of the facebook algorithm). So the free and standard use of Facebook, even if it can give us the feeling of being able to get everywhere, is actually limited: we are "targeting" only our own circle of friends, while the other potentially interested users get lost in the sea of information of the thousands of proposals present.

To remedy this type of operation, commercial pages have been introduced in Facebook, with the aim of allowing the registration of people interested in a certain type of activity and therefore of getting in touch with them directly. Probably other platforms have other artifices or other logics, but the common sense is the same: as for the web page, the problem of appearing in a container where there are a lot of messages, is absolutely a priority to solve. It is not plausible to think that a potential customer sees every single publication or every single ad: here marketing techniques intervene to improve the charm of the ads rather than the effectiveness of the advertising campaigns. The first objective always remains that << the greatest number of people see the existence of their ad and secondly that they decide to read it >> because it has attracted his attention. Let's go back to talking about the landing pages that you can insert in a text ad with the aim of converting that attention received into a sale, or videos or very attractive images that must come to produce the attention of new customers. The big news is that so far we have talked about all this, but practically at no cost (free facebook service), that is in the standard mode: the problem with this type is that it is very limited, because the situation is not the manager has it, but it depends randomly on a customer who decides to subscribe to his page or to his personal circle of friends. Among other things, these potential users are not yet considered as "real customers" because they may simply be curious or not have a specific interest in "buying" (remember that the product, or objective, can be physical, but also simply advertise your company or professionalism). So the conversion rate (ie the ability to transform a contact into a sale) is very low, and we could therefore speak of << a lot of noise for nothing >>, with slight effects on the diffusion of certain messages or of a certain level of advertising ', but absolutely not relevant in positive to create revenues. On the contrary, it could instead attract haters, and then not have the numbers or the strength to be able to deny them and it can be very harmful for our company.

How can social media become a weapon of advantage for a company and produce revenues? The so-called organic publicis a good starting point to measure yourself at the beginning and understand the market logic, but it is not at all sufficient and alone will never produce, as far as it may present high interest numbers, real revenues . To optimize the social tool on a professional level, the only answer is to invest and plan, then marketing.

<< When ever in the history of commerce something that is free produces revenues and earnings? >>. Answer << never! >>, word already included in the question.

If you do not pay you can survive, earn something, but in the vast majority of cases it is totally insufficient to handle the marketing of an entire company. Advertising must be paid for and therefore, remembering the old school models, you just have to be happy to pay so little, but you have to access the paid step, because otherwise you will not advance. Returning to the example of Facebook, there is a paid service which is precisely the Facebook ADS, which are nothing more than taking the same ad and proposing it in a completely different, selected market; depending on the parameters that we will decide, it allows us to get the message to only certain categories. Another great innovation, speaking of the price, is that everyone decides how much to invest for each ad. So big news ', because' now we are aware that by paying a little we can go to decide who gets our announcement and who doesn't: we can discriminate the age, gender, area of residence, the particular interests of this person and therefore direct us to an ideal model customer.

There will be statistical elements to check the progress and quality of your marketing actions and conversion rates, then measure the effectiveness of advertising, which with the old school methods was indecipherable. It is really well done and it is a powerful marketing tool. There is only one small and long-standing old problem << the letter arrives in the mailbox, but seeing that the customer is advertising it throws it away >>: we could therefore also reach the perfect customer, but if we get there with an incorrect message either trivial or not incisive, the effort will have been useless: therefore again to underline the importance of the landing pages or anything we send to our end user: it must be simple but of quality, and differentiate and must convert the action for sale or in the goal that is proposed.

- **YOU TUBE**

  For You Tube, I sincerely feel like making a separate speech and not locking it up in the social category. In a certain sense it is, because people can interact through comments, but on the other hand it was born as a platform for music videos and becomes so popular that it is now converted into the most popular container of any video in the world. In fact, there are now videos of all kinds, from small film clippings to the entire film, from music videos to the complete discography of an author; but pay attention to the absolutely innovative advertising application: this was for example one of the most incisive vehicles of the disclosure of what is ad hoc advertising, that is, the one that comes out of the margin of a daily and normal action, like looking for a song on the internet, and almost unconsciously "pay" it by being subjected to an advertisement at the beginning of the service or appearing to the side during. There are many famous sites, with heavy visitor traffic, where advertising bannersare published, which are the real sponsors of those services. To access it there are ADS payment policies that must necessarily be a marketing study: there are "pay-per clicks"or other devices, for which to personalize a real campaign. And even more interesting is the << intuitive system of interest >>: to date, search engines and cokiees (automatic messages rich in information, which are sent to the search engines on the most visited sites) are now possible advertising campaigns that act << on the interests and memory >> of the virtual navigator. For example, if a person searches on the website of Ikea, the global furniture giant, a product of his online store, this will be classified in some way, and remains in memory, so it is possible that, the result of elaborate campaigns of marketing, we find ourselves the next day reproposed that same object or other similar in some banner, when we go to visit any other site of our interest (sometimes in the same category, but sometimes even in terms of fun or that have nothing to do with see with a purchase). Imagine which advertising channel is more impactful and user-friendly than a film, music and various interests platform like You Tube! So an entrepreneur could intervene at the marketing level by creating intelligent and ultra-modern campaigns with these systems and always discriminating the type of customer, and having control over the number of ads seen and the number of clicks.

In any case, one of the other most interesting uses from a commercial point of view is the so-called Tutoriabr video guide, where sector experts publish videos that are often very useful on **"how to solve a problem":** there are simple cooking videos to the more complex, mechanical; from videos of professionals explaining certain situations to videos of companies explaining the stages of a production.

It is therefore extremely important from a strategic point of view for two main reasons: the first is that a truly capable person can create a video that illustrates his professionalism, and through the tool of offering a free demonstration, accessible to all, attracting new customers. . The second thing is for advertising purposes only to make yourself known, attract a large number of audiences and even in some cases monetize directly from the web, thanks to the great visibility that is then remunerated. In fact, not everyone knows that You Tube is owned by Google (the most important search engine in the world) and therefore its videos are normally highly indexed and pushed if they receive visits, which for Google is synonymous with being interesting.

Google and Facebook, to date, are the two most powerful search barsin the world, because they count with the most detailed information of potential customers and have the best technology available on the market, as well as applications. The problem then, here as before, is to emerge from the chaos of messages and videos uploaded to the platform, and often we find ourselves finding that a beautiful and super interesting video has very few views, at the expense of one made much worse , which covers the same topic and has thousands and thousands of views. So how do you achieve certain results? You Tube, like all platforms, has an interest that its customers are constantly connected, therefore it rewards the amount of videos uploaded: the experts themselves confirm that hardly anyone who publishes a single video can make large numbers: they therefore promote the self-supply of the platform inviting to make videos. This thing, on the one hand attracts very competent people who offer interesting technical or curious videos, artistic expressions and very useful advice. On the other hand, it attracts instead the lust for protagonism of certain other characters, who with the objective of "notoriety" (or with the objective of << doing a job, which they often cannot do >>), produce videos that are totally questionable in terms of quality and content . These subjects obviously lower the average quality of video productions and disperse "the potential to be seen" by others: unfortunately there is no taste filter, so it is obvious that they are the rules of the game. As if this were not enough, the junk videos are very popular and very popular with the public and even almost for a sort of "reverse justice", they tend to get a lot of views, and therefore these characters continue very willingly in their production. Speaking of real estate, for example, this is what happens sometimes with videos of excellent professionals, who make absolutely truthful and useful market surveys, at the expense of someone who "claims to be real estate" and sometimes says quite the opposite, without meaning , and therefore confusing the correct work of the other, moreover. How to combat this phenomenon and make the public understand that it is "the good one"? First of all by investing, because exactly as it happens with Facebook, there is a paid plan to push your production, connected to the Google ADS:then with the strength of the numbers, exhibit a different credibility of your videos (I know it seems a trifle to have to pay to stand in front of someone perhaps inept, but unfortunately freedom and ease of publication has this price). Secondly, there is a keyword strategy that You Tube allows to implement and that reads according to its algorithm. Understanding the keywords to enter to position yourself, so that a possible customer finds us before others, is essential and makes the difference. Thirdly, there is the usual system of reviews and comments that could give indications on good and less good videos, but unfortunately, in this case they are currently filterable, so it is plausible that the subjects we were talking about hide them. Warning: I say that it is very sad, in terms of numbers, because with a sensationalist video, a subject could get to have many clicks, but obviously then a potential customer will watch the video and make an opinion: it is evident that at that point he will understand if the video or the character has no quality (but the click will already be counted), and at this point he will probably interrupt the vision, looking for another more professional one: clearly this strategy brings fame, but does not convert potential customers into real customers. As a professional, I prefer a few qualified and selected clients, who see a video of mine and maybe convert into a real client, rather than having thousands of registered fans, perhaps most disgruntled, who do not lead me to monetize anything even over time. Quality always pays, in the end, and therefore also "who publishes" must then decide what << job to do in life >>: whether the entertainer or the professional; in fact, in the long run, these phenomena tire and people lose interest, or they completely lose credibility when they demonstrate scarce content, or very rough knowledge of the topics covered, or bizarre theories. So personally to companies and investors I recommend quality videos, with marketing techniques applied, not focused on sensationalism, but absolutely professional, aimed at a business purpose, demonstrating the seriousness and goodness of the product. The **advantages** of investing in this type of platform are that, often, it is the user who enters here looking for a solution, and not the company to go looking for it; moreover, the videos are very strong in terms of communication: larger than a photo, but less dispersive than a brochure. In a modern system everything is very visual, and few people read, at least in this type of situation: a quick and impactful solution is sought. They are also modular, being able to vary aside from the topics, the more serious style, the use of audio or subtitles; Finally, let's not forget the advantage and convenience of "showing something" in real time, while the user emulates us on the other side of the screen. If we then learn to invest, use the correct keywordsand invest in ADS, managing to have some fashion videos, our business could take advantage of a visibility that is completely exponential and therefore grow visibly.

- **SALES LIST or CARD:** leaving the internet, I would like to approach something that was part of the old school, but has undergone an absolutely current "re-adaptation" over the years and connects to the aforementioned bar-staging and looking for consistency and homogeneity between the product-point of sale and communication.

From time immemorial a company in any sector has always had a list of its products, and for this reason the issue and the importance of having an order and an interesting variety of products to offer is well known. However, its application is even more interesting, for example in the restaurant sector, where I believe it should be contextualized in a modern concept. In fact, what once represented only << the list of dishes offered in a restaurant >>, today, unless we are talking about elite niches, or family management, must be studied in order to optimize costs - receive, through a study that certainly has in its foundations << the best quality 'at the most accessible price possible >>, to produce large numbers. It must also represent the spirit and character of the store. From this perspective, therefore, composing a good card or list becomes a marketing action, and not just an instrumental and practical use of a list. The greatest cheffs /television entrepreneurs, in their dedicated thematic programs, when they go to propose a "change of image of a local", also and above all work on the "paper", with attention to the demand / offer, to the capacity of the point sale of being able to express a certain production, with price logics, with novelty and contextualization logics on the site: if we think in England of Gordon Ramsey (from the "Cucine dell'Inferno" program) and in Spain of Alberto Chicote ("Pesadilla en la cocina"), are two connoisseurs, who with a very professional team intervene on the premises from an aesthetic, marketing and therefore also and above all by changing the product offer, to give a new personality to the various catering sites. Among other things, we remember that "this is my personal specialization", and for this I collaborate with sites like www.bares360.es where precisely this type of marketing and services is promoted.

Anyone can study a "card"; but studying a card that can convert into sales, to optimize revenues is a much more elaborate and complex job, exactly like all the other techniques analyzed so far, which are available to everyone in a free or intuitive way, but certainly have a different "firepower" if a professional uses them.

- **ORGANIZATION OF EVENTS AS A MARKETING PLAN:** previously we had proposed the example of a room with an entertainment room, which organizes events, with a precise strategy of increasing the turnout and brand value. Most companies use events for the sole purpose of attracting people and making themselves known, or increasing revenue at certain punctual moments. But seen from a commercial perspective, it is necessary to think that every single fan of an artist or a show can convert into a potential real customer, and in turn generate new customer flows once loyal, because he will recommend us to others. Seen in this light therefore there are very interesting commercial choices to be made on the style of the shows, rather than on the names of the artists and obviously the cost: in fact, each typology could have a different audience for economic availability or age, and therefore it is interesting use the organization of events to plan a growth strategy over time aimed at training a certain type of customer, akin to our business, and not only use it as a mere "one-night" in order to make an interesting collection. In these cases, there is also a need to reflect on ticket payment policies and services and accessory spaces to generate revenues: the location of the food area, the beverage area, for example. Sometimes I happened to see in my long experience of the premises, perfect concerts full of people, but that the organizer was unable to convert correctly into sales, due to lack of organization, because overwhelmed by the unexpected number of users, for the incorrect arrangement of the sensitive points to join the collection. It is therefore very important to plan something that attracts the public, to study what kind of audience then and how to be able to optimize revenues by giving them the main service and the accessory ones, and all this aimed at both making a great income, but also cultivating something important over time, which replicated, which increases the value of the company and the brand.

- **HUMAN RESOURCES AS A SOURCE OF MARKETING:** all of us have happened to walk through a commercial area and find young people who come close and offer us to visit a place to sell products: the classic PR public relations, that promote the store in the street or in the more advanced form of the night that organize parties and events in discos, moving quantities of people and bringing them to the store. The lowest common denominator is "attracting attention" and is the best known and most widespread form of human resource marketing. Obviously, these supports have a cost and can be more or less valid, depending on the period, the capabilities and what you want to promote. However, there are other human resources suitable for promoting a shop that in a certain sense could do so without increasing costs: the employees. In fact, employees are one of the natural sources of corporate marketing, as they are often "the face that speaks to the public" and therefore they are in all respects the subjects who must send absolutely positive messages and aligned with the style of the company in which they work. Let's think for a moment about what a powerful marketing action is << wearing a uniform with the company logo >> for each employee. Creating uniforms of this kind, at the beginning, appears to be an avoidable cost, but in the end it is a very forward-looking marketing operation because customers constantly display the company logo and it remains etched in the mind, and people passing by (think of the example of a promenade) they see the logo, maybe the smile of those who represent the company and they remember and maybe they are attracted to try the experience. Then we think of "word of mouth" and the friendships of the employees themselves: these can, with their good work, ensure that a company has the constant sap of customers, who are loyal to the good work done by the person who exercises in the store. On the contrary, it is clear that this can negatively affect when you have unmotivated or even incapable employees. So also the selection of human resources, by gender, age, ability, attitude, can be an important marketing choice because it produces direct consequences at work and indirect from the point of view of communication that in the long run affect the store's revenue. There has always been the old balance of imbalance between employee and employee, and sometimes one or the other have complaints about the other party: finding the perfect balance is a difficult business programming action, which but it is necessary: therefore, flexibility is needed on both sides, for a single common purpose, which is that of the corporate good. In fact, both when things are going well have "to gain". If instead they go wrong, probably everyone has to lose.

We never underestimate this type of marketing, because it is fundamental, and above all a good employee applies it in a natural way just by doing his job well, so it is absolutely not an additional cost. (A bad employee on the contrary generates losses and problems).

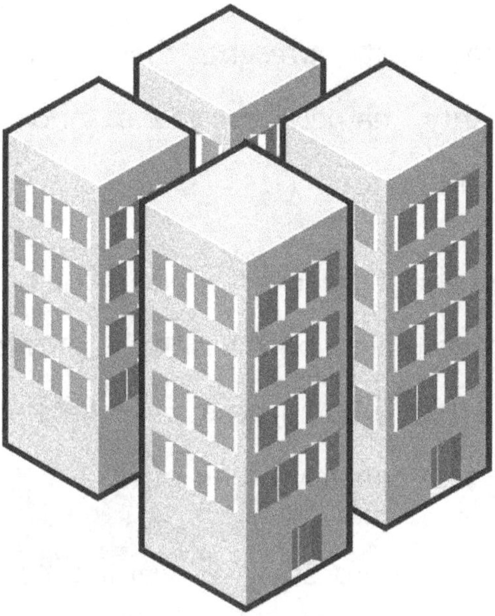

It doesn't matter if you take the best photos or videos if nobody sees them!

CONCLUSIONS

During our analysis we dealt with all aspects concerning residential and commercial investments, with special attention in the latter case to commercial activities and the category that most represents them in terms of diffusion and popularity, namely the food and beverage and revenueinment sector.

So we talked about the investor and all he needs to know to buy well and build a business that is profitable and that can provide him with income over time, differentiating unstable investments from safer ones.

Throughout this process, we wanted to underline the importance of programming, of serious and devoted application to the business system, conducted in a non-casual form, but inspired by good ideas, supported by facts and professional actions, aimed at increasing a make it strong and useful. We then definitely defined the do-it-yourself, intended as improvisation, an attempt to save or disorder, as a very widespread, but very negative element since in the long run it does not allow to build the foundations for stable and profitable work, giving only a few benefits immediately, and on the contrary, often generating a series of problems and inconsistencies that lead the company to make less than hoped for.

On the contrary we have promoted the action of a few but good professionals of the various professions: it is not secondary to differentiate the really good ones from the mediocre ones, but once done, we have motivated what are the important values that these professional figures should have, and above all done a portrait of how an investor can recognize and evaluate them and the knowledge they should have.

Because... let's not forget that the common goal of all this path is that of the company asset and the optimization of the investment, so you must know how to recognize the right investment, be able to grab it, mount a system that is profitable and succeed to sell: a lot of specializations required, therefore, for a very long laborious and complex job, which if it runs smoothly in any of these phases, turns into less profitable than expected, even to the point of being negative. In this sense, we find at the end, the real difference between the do it yourselfand a professional support system for an investor: provided that both situations can lead to success or failure, as the case may be, what is certain that a self-styled allologist who "arranges himself" can only go so far; but an entrepreneur with vision and organization, who knows how to make use of his knowledge, and where he wants to optimize his revenues, with the help of valid professional advice, always has an additional weapon, as well as a meter of comparison. Indeed, I would say that this is precisely the point: it will be able to express a clearly more targeted and broader firepower, and it will certainly achieve the objectives it had set itself and perhaps even go further.

CPSIA information can be obtained
at www.ICGtesting.com
Printed in the USA
BVHW070952200421
605389BV00005B/1614

9 781802 358810